# *The History of Accounting*

*This is a volume in the Arno Press collection*

# *The History of Accounting*



*See last pages of this volume*
*for a complete list of titles*

THE

# DEPRECIATION OF FACTORIES

## MINES AND INDUSTRIAL UNDERTAKINGS

## AND THEIR VALUATION

BY

EWING MATHESON

ARNO PRESS
A New York Times Company
New York — 1976

Editorial Supervision: SHEILA MEHLMAN

Reprint Edition 1976 by Arno Press Inc.

Reprinted from a copy in The American Institute
of Certified Public Accountants Library

THE HISTORY OF ACCOUNTING
ISBN for complete set: 0-405-07540-5
See last pages of this volume for titles.

Manufactured in the United States of America

Publisher's Note: The frontispiece has been reproduced in black and white for this edition.

Library of Congress Cataloging in Publication Data

Matheson, Ewing.
The depreciation of factories, mines, and industrial undertakings and their valuation.

Reprint of the 1893 ed. published by E. & F. N. Spon, London.
1. Depreciation. 2. Factories--Accounting. 3. Factories--Valuation. I. Title. II. Series.
HF5681.D5M4 1976 657'.42 75-18476
ISBN 0-405-07558-8

# THE DEPRECIATION OF FACTORIES

## MINES AND INDUSTRIAL UNDERTAKINGS

AND

## THEIR VALUATION

EXAMPLE OF

# THE DEPRECIATION OF A FACTORY IN 30 YEARS.

For Explanation see Page 56.

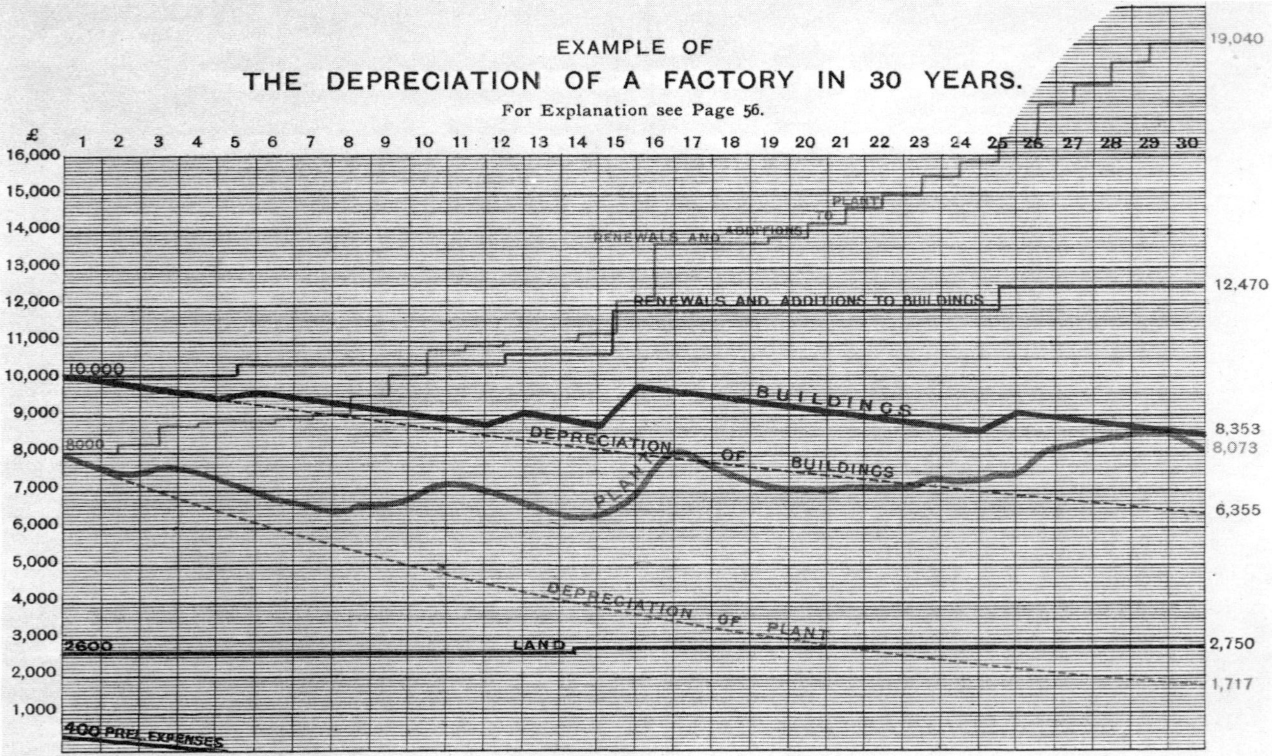


| | Value in 1st Year. | | 30th Year. |
|---|---|---|---|
| Buildings .............. | £10,000 | ............ | £8,353 |
| Plant .................... | 8,000 | ............ | 8,073 |
| Land ..................... | 2,600 | ............ | 2,750 |
| Prel. Expenses ...... | 400 | ............ | — |
| Total... | £21,000 | ............ | £19,176 |

THE

# DEPRECIATION OF FACTORIES

## MINES AND INDUSTRIAL UNDERTAKINGS

## AND THEIR VALUATION

BY

EWING MATHESON

M. INST. C.E.

*SECOND EDITION*

London:

E. & F. N. SPON, 125 STRAND

New York:

SPON & CHAMBERLAIN, 12 CORTLANDT STREET

1893

# PREFACE.

In the Financial administration of a Factory or other industrial undertaking, the Accounts which relate to Disbursements and Receipts are so obviously necessary to the continuous working of the undertaking as to be rarely neglected, and if errors or omissions occur, they quickly compel attention. But the Capital accounts are not always deemed to be of such pressing importance, and variations in the value of plant arising from the wear and tear may be left unnoted. The increasing extent of Factories, the subdivision of capital by means of joint-stock companies, and the conflicting interests that arise in regard to preference shares and borrowed capital, enhance greatly the importance of correct systems of account. Qualified book-keepers should be employed to arrange and check factory accounts, and the profession of Accountant and Auditor is rising in importance accordingly. But while Accountants may properly deal with facts and figures presented to them, and may fairly allot to Capital and Revenue actual expenditure or Estimated Depreciation, they must always be dependent for the accuracy of these *data* on those technically acquainted with the operations of manufacture. It is endeavoured in the present short treatise to point out the leading circumstances that must be considered in "Writing off" for Depreciation, and to tabulate in a simple manner the annual changes that occur in Capital value.

In the Valuation of a Factory for any purpose whatever, the past "depreciations" and additions have to be considered, and the possible modifications which may be necessary are dealt with in the later chapters.

The first four chapters have already appeared in the *Engineer*, from September to November 1883, but have been revised and extended here.

LONDON, 1884.

---

## *PREFACE TO THE SECOND EDITION.*

THE various criticisms and suggestions by accountants, manufacturers, and others on the principles enunciated in this treatise as it first appeared, have led the Author to revise it when a new edition was called for. The writing off the diminishing or wasting value of Terminable undertakings has been dealt with, the provision afforded by Leasehold Assurance is described, and the rates of premium given. Some new points connected with collieries and ironworks are also referred to.

LONDON, 1893.

# INTRODUCTION

TO

# THE SECOND EDITION.

BY WILLIAM CHARLES JACKSON,

*Mem. Council Inst. Chartered Accountants.*

THE value to the professional Accountant of a standard work on the subject of Depreciation cannot easily be over-estimated. Few of the persons in whose interest his services as an auditor are employed, are fully competent to appreciate that profits of manufacture are not gained until the loss by the wearing out of the machinery of production is provided for; while many of those who conduct the affairs of Companies are unwilling to acknowledge the necessity of such provision, where apparent profits are cut down and dividends thereby diminished.

The principles of Depreciation, and its incidence under varying circumstances, are clearly laid down in Mr. Matheson's work; and the guidance, which, as his preface says, must be sought from those technically acquainted with the operations of manufacture, is to be found lucidly expressed in his pages.

To those who honestly and from conviction treat the subject on the only sound basis, it may seem superfluous to urge due consideration of the arguments so convincingly set out in these pages; but Auditors, and especially those who have to deal with joint-stock or other concerns where the remuneration of the management is made wholly or partly dependent upon declared Profits, know in what varied forms resistance to an adequate Charge against profits for Depreciation is presented.

The fallacies underlying these objections present themselves again and again with the modifications caused by the lack of apprehension in some, or the ingenuity of others. Mr. Matheson's work provides the Auditor with true antidotes to these fallacies, and it has been in past times used by the writer with satisfactory effect, where his own less-reasoned arguments have failed to convince.

He therefore recommends it afresh to the notice and for the support, where necessary, of members of his own profession, and of those who, untrained in the practice of Auditing, are confronted with unfamiliar and specious pretexts for avoiding the unwelcome charge against Profits.

# CONTENTS.

## PART I.

## DEPRECIATION.

### CHAPTER I.



### CHAPTER II.



### CHAPTER III.



### CHAPTER IV.



### CHAPTER V.



### CHAPTER VI.

## PART II.

## VALUATION.

# PART I.

# DEPRECIATION.

## CHAPTER I.

### THE GENERAL PRACTICE OF DEPRECIATION.

THE Deterioration of a Factory by time and use, the appraisement of the loss and its allotment in the accounts of the undertaking, are matters of great importance in the economy of management; and any neglect or error in "writing off" will, according to its extent, render calculations of cost and profit fallacious. No fixed rules, or rates of depreciation can be established for general use, because not only do trades and processes of manufacture differ, but numerous secondary circumstances have to be considered in determining the proper course. It may, however, be possible to lay down some general principles which will always apply, or which, at any rate, may with advantage be held in view in deciding particular cases.

**Fixed rules cannot be established.**

The question of depreciation cannot be separated from that of maintenance, and in theory one may be said to balance the other. In practice it is only in certain cases that this can be acted on. In any particular building, machine, or appurtenance, decay or wear of some sort must take place in the course of time, and repairs, in order to compensate fully for the decline in value, must take the form of renewal. This being the case, the absolute replacement of some portion of the plant every year may

**Depreciation and maintenance.**

thus maintain an average aggregate value. In only two kinds or classes of plant, however, can such an exact balancing of loss by repairs and renewals be ventured on; one, where the plant wears out so quickly as to need replacement at short intervals, affording constant proof, by the mere continuance of working, that not only the earning power of the factory is maintained, but also the capital value; and in a second class, that of undertakings so large and permanent as to afford a wide average of deterioration and renewal over the whole plant.

**Renewals may balance loss.**

*See page* 48.

For instance, on a Railway the deterioration of the fixed and moving plant is supposed to be fully and properly met by the expenditure for repairs and renewals, and so long as the working of the railway is maintained, no regard is had to a future valuation such as might disturb the accounts of a manufactory subject to a change of ownership or cessation of trade. When a railway has been in operation for many years, and an average rate of expenditure in relation to revenue has been arrived at, such a method may be sound, but there is a risk that in the earlier years of working the gross revenue may not be sufficiently charged with due depreciation.

**Railway renewals.**

**Average rates.**

Railway companies in England have to publish annual accounts in a form prescribed by law, but these accounts seldom fully disclose the deterioration of the plant, partly because the expenditure of a particular year for repairs or renewals may not represent the deterioration due to the traffic of that year, and partly because expenditure necessary for maintenance may be mixed up with the capital expenditure for extensions.

**Railway accounts.**

**Maintenance charged to capital.**

There is often a natural tendency to write off for depreciation in proportion to the profits, rather than to the deterioration; and yet a large portion of the plant of a railway affords by its uniformity facilities for analysis which are wanting in most private manufactories. The

Permanent way, for instance, by its extent, generally allows of trustworthy averages ; the Locomotives also, being composed of essential parts of a uniform kind, the annual expense due to wear and tear is ascertainable without much difficulty after a few years of working. Results can be so tabulated * and compared with the traffic of a particular period as to allow the establishment of fixed rules concerning the cost of maintenance due to special causes, *e.g.* altered kinds of traffic, increased mileage, and alterations in speed.

**Analysis of expenditure.**

But while such conspicuous and essential expenditure as that for the maintenance of permanent way and rolling-stock cannot be ignored, the Workshops of a railway, in which much of the expenditure takes place, form an adjunct of an indefinite character, where no such precise proportion of annual expenditure to traffic is established. Railways differ in regard to their workshops, some companies making engines as well as repairing them, and it is not always easy to separate and allot the expenditure and establishment charges due to new work and to repairs. Some railway companies, however, go much farther than others in the analysis of their workshop accounts.

**Railway workshops.**

**Cost of making and repairing not easily separated.**

Indirectly the varying value of railway workshops is manifested from time to time by the assessments for purposes of Rating, which are made upon railways in common with all other real property. From this point of view a low valuation is in the interest of the company, and deterioration by time and wear has periodically to be considered to ascertain how far it balances additions and renewals.

**Rating valuation.**

*See page* 105.

The omission of any provision in the earlier years for future renewals is often excused by the small earnings, but the wear and tear necessary to such earnings must

**Provision for renewals.**

* See "The Maintenance and Renewal of Railway Rolling Stock," by R. Price Williams, M. Inst. C.E. 'Minutes of Proceedings of the Institution of Civil Engineers,' vol. xxx., Session 1869–70.

sooner or later be paid for out of revenue or from new capital; and though in course of years the expenditure for repairs and renewals must almost of necessity balance the deterioration if the traffic is to go on, there is room for much error in the accounts of particular years; and in the case of constantly changing shareholders, of an unfair allotment of charges. The writing off of preliminary expenses is dealt with in a later chapter.

**Unfair to changing owners.** *See pages* 26, 56.

In Great Britain, although there is a natural and unavoidable tendency to increase the capital of a railway as a provision for growing traffic, the original works are generally of a substantial kind to meet the statutory requirements of Government inspectors. All subsequent expenditure that does not increase the earning capacity of the line should be treated as maintenance and be defrayed out of revenue. This principle may however be carried too far, as is illustrated by the system of "betterment" adopted on some American railways. In providing new communications, especially between districts far apart, the utmost economy is practised, everything being postponed that is not immediately necessary to the running of trains. Not only may there be little or no outlay for land and for charters, but there may be omitted at the outset ballast, fences, over-bridges, signals and stations. Some or all of these are added after a line is opened, but it does not always suit the purpose or interest of those who control the line to raise fresh capital. Where, therefore, there is available revenue after paying current working charges, a considerable part of such surplus is applied to betterment instead of to the payment of dividend to the shareholders. This system, though it is sounder than the opposite extreme of unduly increasing the capital, may be nevertheless unfair to existing shareholders who are tantalised by the anomaly of favourable traffic returns and large revenue with little or no dividend. In Great

**Railway capital.**

**"Betterment" on American railways.**

**Cheap construction.**

**Revenue spent on improvements.**

Britain, however, it is the opposite extreme that has to be guarded against.

**Surplus income treated as profit,**

The temptation to treat as Profit the Surplus of Income over Expenditure, without sufficient allowance for Deterioration, appears to be often irresistible. Thus, in the case of a Tramway undertaking in its first years of working, a dividend may be possible only by writing off little or nothing from the capital value of the cars, the harness, and the horses. This, of course, cannot last without the introduction of new capital, but in undertakings long established there yet may be epochs of fictitious profits due to various causes. For instance there may be neglect of repairs, which, when the necessity for them becomes evident, will involve a heavy outlay for renewals ; or it may arise from actual fraud in postponing expenditure, so as to show large profits, which will raise the value of shares for stock-jobbing purposes. There are railways where the dividend income and the corresponding value of the shares have fluctuated considerably, not according to alterations in the real earnings, but according to alternate neglect and attention in regard to plant.

*See also page* 53.

**without regard to provision for depreciation.**

**Fictitious profits.**

In industrial undertakings, so long as additions and extensions are being made which absorb the capital rendered free by a system of depreciation, shareholders may recognise that such an application of part of the profits saves them from having to find new capital. But where capital outlay is not continuous, and an actual fund is accumulating in money for future contingencies more or less remote, shareholders are frequently unwilling to see such money invested outside their own undertaking.

**Investment of reserve.**

*See page* 21.

**Water companies' accounts.**

Water-supply companies afford another example of permanent undertakings where deterioration of plant is not always dealt with in the accounts. It is not usual to write off in the annual accounts, as presented to the shareholders, anything for depreciation, but renewals as well as repairs

**Provision for renewals.**

are effected out of the current revenue. In very large and long-established undertakings an average expenditure will eventually be arrived at, which, as in the case of railways, serves instead of a depreciation rate, by charging the earnings of each year. But in the earlier years of working, when expenditure for renewals has not commenced, the earnings are often divided as profit, without setting apart a reserve for the replacement of the plant.

**Renewals neglected in earlier years.**

In the case of water companies with a capital not exceeding £100,000, the expenditure for renewals occurs at irregular intervals; but instead of providing by anticipation for such outlays, it is more usual to open a "Suspense account," after the expenditure has been incurred—as, for instance, for a new pumping engine or boilers—and to divide the cost over a subsequent term of years. Of course, when this system has become well established, and suspense accounts are always running, the effect on any particular year's income will probably not differ much from that of a regular depreciation rate, but the apparent profit of the earlier years has been increased at the expense of later years. A suspense account may be best opened before the actual expenditure occurs; it would then be usually called a Reserve fund.

**Suspense accounts.**

**Reserve fund.** *See page* 60.

**Indirect reserve fund.**

In many companies, however, even where no direct provision for repairs and renewals is made, there is an indirect reserve. Water-supply companies are in this country almost always established by Act of Parliament, and the mode of keeping accounts and dividing profits is to some extent prescribed. Subject to occasional modification in the special Acts authorising particular companies, the conditions generally are those of the Waterworks Companies Clauses Consolidation Acts of 1845 and 1877, which allow, in the discretion of the directors, a reserve fund to be set apart out of profits to equalise dividends in any future years, when current profits do not allow the

**Dividends equalised.**

maximum dividend permitted by the special Act of the company, the reserve fund being limited to one-tenth of the capital. This reserve fund can only be applied to its prescribed purpose of equalising dividends, and cannot be used directly for repairs; but it is obvious that if the earnings of a particular year are burdened with some heavy expenditure for renewals, the latter are really paid for out of the fund nominally applicable for dividend. But the establishment of such reserve funds is seldom authorised by shareholders, except out of surplus earnings beyond 5 or 6 per cent., and therefore in the case of struggling or unremunerative companies the renewals are all charged forward. The unsoundness of the system may be disguised; but it is one which, when adopted in private undertakings, is frequently a cause of illusion and failure. In the case of prosperous companies with large net revenue, and whose monopoly assures a continuance of profits, repairs and renewals are carried out liberally; and in cases where the rate of dividend is limited by law, there is even a tendency to overstate the expenditure on this account, so as to disguise the real net profit, and postpone a reduction in the price of water which profits beyond a certain limit might render obligatory.

**Limitation of reserve fund.**

**Renewals charged forward.**

**Excessive profits disguised.**

With Gas-supply companies also, a reserve fund for renewals is not always established, and though in one sense they are permanent undertakings, they have not so secure a future as in the case of water companies. Moreover the plant used in the manufacture and distribution of gas differs from that used in water supply—more of it being of a kind to wear out rapidly. Retorts and other parts of the plant of short endurance are renewed out of current revenue, and with due care these charges bear a fixed proportion to the earnings; but when some considerable renewal takes place and only the part which extends the earning capacity is defrayed out of new capital, the remainder of the outlay,

**Gas companies' accounts.**

**Deterioration of plant.**

which only makes good the wear and tear of the past, tells most unfairly on the current year's income. A postponement of the charge to future years is equally unsatisfactory, if the deterioration which has called for it is really due to the work of preceding years. But, as in the case of water companies, if the profits are large and the dividends are restricted to a maximum, the expenditure out of revenue for repairs and renewals, and even for what really are extensions, is sometimes very lavish, and the accounts may be as fictitious in this direction as in the reverse cases above alluded to. Legislation, however, has been directed towards the ensuring of a fairer system, increased dividends being permitted only in proportion as the price of gas is reduced. The interests of the consumers and the shareholders are thus rendered more nearly identical, so far as economy in management is concerned.

**Renewals unduly allotted.**

**Lavish renewals out of profits.**

**Profits limited by law.**

**Renewals may balance deterioration.**

In the case of very large manufactories, where there is a considerable annual outlay for renewals of plant as well as for repairs, such expenditure, if charged to revenue, may fairly balance the average deterioration of the whole. But to secure this, there should be an ample margin—say by an obvious increase of the plant every year—for without this there will be a risk that a gradual lessening of the total value of buildings or plant will take place, ultimately involving considerable expenditure to restore its earning capacity. There may be neglect of due provision for deterioration in a new factory without any warning sign, while everything is in full working order. It is true, as in the case of the railway just cited, the earnings may be undeveloped, and no fund available from which to provide for future repairs, but the omission is none the less unsound.

*See page* 14.

**Risk of neglect in new factories.**

**Tendency of factories to increase.**

It is seldom that any large manufactory can be successful without Extensions of plant, but an increase in capital value cannot be properly assumed unless the earning power is increased in a corresponding ratio and the shortened life of the plant due to past use duly provided for. In the accounts of a factory it is difficult even for those engaged in its management always to distinguish between the expenditure for renewals chargeable to capital and that due to deterioration; and to those outside the management it is quite impossible without careful investigation rarely attempted. Of course, actual additions to the size of a factory may be duly reckoned as increasing the fixed capital; but such an increase may be wholly or partially neutralised by the deterioration of the older part. It may be said that the success of many undertakings, and their survival through the vicissitudes of dull times and during radical alterations in trade, have been due to the liberal charging of extentions to revenue.

**Difficulty in allotting charges.**

*See Frontispiece, also page* 56.

But while manufacturers may deduct from the value of their plant the estimated loss by wear and tear, and must in prudence apply part of their earnings to make good the loss in the capital account, the Law only partially recognises such a deduction from profits in calculating Income tax. Up to the year 1878 no allowance whatever was permitted, and in the year 1876 the principle of this refusal was confirmed by the following test case tried before three Judges in the Exchequer Division of the High Court of Justice:—

**Deductions for renewal**

**not allowed in income tax.**

"FORDER *v.* ANDREW HANDYSIDE AND COMPANY (LIMITED).*

**Case of Forder against Handyside.**

"A sum set aside out of the net profits of a company, under the articles of association, for the purpose of meeting the depreciation of buildings, fixed plant, and machinery, is in the nature of capital, and cannot be deducted from the profits liable to income tax under Schedule D.

"This was a case stated under 37 & 38 Vict. c. 16, ss. 8 & 9, for the opinion of the Court, in the matter of an appeal of Andrew Handyside and Co. (Limited), against an assessment to income tax under

* 'Law Journal Reports' (New Series), vol. 45, Common Law, p. 809.

Schedule D made to the Commisioners for the district of Morleston and Litchurch, Derbyshire.

**Case stated.**

"Andrew Handyside and Company (Limited) were assessed under Schedule D, for the year 1874-5, at £8642, the amount stated in their report as net profits. In the report for the year ending 31st July, 1874, being their first year of trading, £1509 7*s*. 6*d*., part of this sum, was described as 'amount written off for depreciation of buildings, fixed plant and machinery.'

**Part of gross profit set apart for depreciation.**

"This sum of £1509 7*s*. 6*d*. was written off from the net profits, in accordance with the articles of association, by which (Art. 138) the directors were empowered 'from time to time, before recommending any dividend, to set aside out of the net profits of the company, such sum as they think proper, as a reserve fund for the purpose of meeting contingencies, or of purchasing, improving, enlarging, rebuilding, restoring, reinstating, or maintaining the works, plant, and other premises or property of the company, or in furtherance of any objects of the company, and the same may be applied accordingly, from time to time, in such manner as the directors may determine. The reserve fund, or such part thereof for the time being as is not invested as hereinafter provided, may be used for the general purposes of the company. The interest of the reserve fund shall be treated as annual profits of the company.'

**Appealed against by Surveyor of Taxes.**

"The majority of the Commissioners being of opinion 'that persons in trade were equitably entitled to write off from their profits such a sum for depreciation, and that the amount claimed was fair and reasonable,' decided in favour of the company. The Surveyor of Taxes, being dissatisfied with this decision, requested that the present case should be stated for the opinion of the Court, whether the company should be allowed the deduction of the £1509 7*s*. 6*d*. claimed by them for depreciation.

**Deductions from profits for repairs**

**limited to an average of past three years.**

"The statute 5 & 6 Vict. c. 35, Schedule D, imposes income tax upon the annual profits or gains arising from any profession, trade, employment, or vocation, and by s. 100 (1st case, 3rd rule), it is provided that 'in estimating the balance of profits and gains chargeable under Schedule D, or for the purpose of assessing the duty thereon, no sum shall be set against or deducted from, or allowed to be set against or deducted from such profits or gains, on account of any sum expended for repairs of premises occupied for the purpose of such trade, manufacture, adventure, or concern, nor for any sum expended for the supply of repairs or alterations of any implements, utensils or articles employed for the purpose of such trade, manufacture, adventure, or concern, beyond the sum usually expended for such purposes, according to an average of three years preceding the year in which such assessment shall be made, nor on account of loss not connected with or arising out of such trade, manufacture, adventure, or concern, nor on account of any capital withdrawn therefrom, nor for any sum employed in improvement of premises occupied for the purpose of such trade, manufacture, adventure, or concern, nor on account or under pretence of any interest which might have been made on such sums if laid out at interest, nor for any debts, except bad debts proved to be such to the satisfaction of the Commissioners respectively, nor for any average loss beyond the actual amount of loss after adjustment, nor for any sum recoverable under an insurance or contract of indemnity.'

"The case having been argued on both sides, the Court gave a unanimous judgment for the Crown, and the deduction for depreciation was disallowed."

**Effect of the above decision.**

It will be seen from the statute recited in the foregoing case, that actual expenditure on repairs and renewals may be deducted from the gross earnings, if they do not exceed "what is usually expended for such purposes during an average of three years preceding," but that according to the decision of the Judges, Income tax was legally chargeable on money reserved to make good deterioration which had already occurred but which as yet had not demanded actual renewals.

**The law altered in 1878.**

The above decision manifested so clearly a need for an alteration in the law, that in the Customs and Inland Revenue Act of 1878 (41 Vict. chap. 15, section 12) it was enacted:—

**Provision as to deduction for depreciation of machinery or plant.**

"12. Notwithstanding any provision to the contrary contained in any Act relating to income tax, the Commissioners for general or special purposes shall, in assessing the profits or gains of any trade, manufacture, adventure, or concern in the nature of trade, chargeable under Schedule D, or the profits of any concern chargeable by reference to the rules of that schedule, allow such deduction as they may think just and reasonable as representing the diminished value by reason of wear and tear during the year of any machinery or plant used for the purposes of the concern, and belonging to the person or company by whom the concern is carried on; and for the purpose of this provision, where machinery or plant is let to the person or company by whom the concern is carried on upon such terms that the person or company is bound to maintain the machinery or plant, and deliver over the same in good condition at the end of the term of the lease, such machinery or plant shall be deemed to belong to such person or company.

"And where any machinery or plant is let upon such terms that the burden of maintaining and restoring the same falls upon the lessor, he shall be entitled, on claim made to the Commissioners for general or special purposes in the manner prescribed by section sixty-one of the Act of the fifth and sixth years of Her Majesty's reign, chapter thirty-five, to have repaid to him such a portion of the sum which may have been assessed and charged in respect to the machinery or plant, and deducted by the lessee on payment of the rent, as shall represent the income tax upon such an amount as the said Commissioners may think just and reasonable, as representing the diminished value by reason of wear and tear of such machinery or plant during the year: Provided that no such claim shall be allowed unless it shall be made within twelve calendar months after the expiration of the year of assessment."

**Allowance to lessor who maintains plant.**

It is to be observed that the above Act provides only for an allowance in regard to the depreciation of Machinery and Plant, and entirely excludes Buildings, so that the profits made in a frail structure which will last only ten years are as fully taxed (although the actual current expenditure for repairs is allowed) as those earned in a solid building having a durability of fifty years. It will be seen also that the decision of the Commisioners as to the amount to be allowed is left without appeal.

*See page* 50.

**Sinking fund for wasting properties.**

Industrial works or undertakings may diminish or waste in value because they are limited in extent or time, but where part of the annual profits is applied to the establishing of a sinking fund for getting back the capital invested in such undertakings, the reduction in the profits is not allowed by the Income Tax Commissioners. In the case of a mine acquired by the payment of a capital sum for the minerals instead of, or in addition to, an annual or tonnage royalty on the mineral gotten, the attempt has been made to deduct from the profits assessable to Income tax the annual reduction in capital value which takes place by the exhaustion of the minerals. This was permitted in the well-known case of Knowles *v.* McAdam,* but was after-

**Not allowed income tax.**

**Collieries.**

*See page* 52.

* Exchequer Division, January 23rd and December 5th, 1877, Knowles and others *v.* McAdam.

wards disallowed when a supposed contrary decision was given on appeal in the case of the Coltness Iron Co. *v.* Black.* There, the sum claimed as a deduction from the assessment did not represent the cost of pit sinking during the year, but the sum arrived at by calculating 2*s.* a ton on iron made, and 1½*d.* a ton on coal sold during the year; it being estimated that this would properly represent the amount of capital expended on making bores and sinking pits which had been exhausted by the year's working. The cost of such sinking was charged in the books of the company to an account called "Sunk Capital Account," and was written off annually by a sum computed at the respective rates above specified, on the quantities of iron made and coal sold in the year, as representing the capital expended on pit sinking, exhausted by the year's working. The effect of the judgment is that no allowance from this provision is made in calculating Income tax, nor can a deduction be made if the sum set apart is as "depreciation" to provide funds for the sinking of new shafts to replace those which are becoming useless as the minerals are consumed. **Legal decisions**

The word "depreciation" being generally applied to the physical deterioration or wear and tear of machinery, the loss by waste in cases like the above should be clearly separated in putting forward a claim for allowance from Income tax. And, in regard to decisions of the Courts, previous cases should not be too readily accepted as precedents unless the circumstances are quite alike. Although the Income Tax Commissioners alleged that the Coltness Case overruled that of Knowles, this has not (1893) been affirmed by the Courts. The Coltness Co. wished to charge the cost of sinking new pits for replacing old ones to revenue, but it has not been decided that a mine owner shall not in any case be entitled to an allowance in respect **Legal precedents.**

* House of Lords. Appeal, April 7th, 1881, from the Court of Session. The Coltness Iron Co. *v.* Black.

of the cost of sinking a pit by means of which pit minerals are gotten which are the source of profit for the year in which the pit is sunk.

**The object of depreciation.** There are various methods of estimating the Depreciation of a Factory, and of recording alteration in Value, but it may be said in regard to any of them that the object in view is so to treat the nominal capital in the books of account, that it shall always represent as nearly as possible the real value. The most effectual method of securing this would be, if it were feasible, to Revalue everything at stated intervals, and to write off whatever loss such valuations might reveal without regard to any prescribed rate. By such a plan the deterioration due to a period of arduous working, or to any average or idle year, would be properly allotted.

**Periodical valuation.**

Such a system is adopted oftenest in factories where the trade and plant are of so simple or uniform a kind as to allow it without difficulty. In some manufactories there are a few chief items of plant which are more important than the rest, and whose condition and value therefore need special consideration. Thus an iron-smelter may directly estimate each year the value of his blast furnaces and blowing engines, and for the miscellaneous or subsidiary plant be content to write a percentage off the original cost without a very close examination. On the other hand iron-smelters sometimes establish a reserve fund—say of 9*d.* or 1*s.* per ton of pig-iron made, and apply the fund to the maintenance and renewal of the whole plant of the furnaces.

**Where adopted.**

**Chief items of plant valued.**

**Blast furnaces.**

The plan of valuing every year instead of adopting a depreciation rate, though it is the more perfect, if strictly carried out, has some disadvantages. The two leading considerations in such an appraisement are generally the condition of the machine or other appurtenance, and its earning power. In both these respects there may be absolutely no

**Valuation difficult.**

sign of deterioration; a machine may appear and for all practical purposes be as good as new, and may show proof of it by actual earnings. Yet none the less its working life is shortening every year, and unless some provision is made for a replacement a severe loss will fall on the future. And if, with this in view, something is written off the value, though no alteration is apparent, then the plan of a depreciation rate is really adopted.

**Where there is no sign of depreciation.**

Manufacturers who abstain in the earlier years of working from writing off depreciation, because they may see no signs of a lessened value, might find it difficult to obtain the full value from an assurance company, in the case of destruction by Fire.

**Fire insurance.** *See page* 99.

For the above reasons, and because of the time, trouble and expense it would involve, a system of annual valuation is seldom strictly maintained; and even where a balance of profit and loss is duly struck every year, an annual valuation of the plant may be deemed impracticable. The next best plan, which is that generally followed, and which it is intended now to investigate, is to establish average rates which can, without much trouble, be written off every year, and to check the result by complete or partial valuation at longer intervals.

**Annual valuation seldom adopted.**

**Average rates of depreciation.**

Before dealing in detail with the various kinds of property in a factory, and attempting to set up a mode of treatment and rate of depreciation appropriate to each, there are certain preliminary questions that need attention. First, the value of any building, plant or apparatus, or aggregation of them, may be largely affected by circumstances outside of their physical condition, and it may be convenient at the outset to separate such circumstances from the wear and tear due to actual use. Among such circumstances are the Tenure under which the factory is occupied; the Permanency or steadiness of profitable em-

**Deterioration other than by wear and tear.**

*See page* 16.
*See page* 50.

ployment which may be anticipated; the exhaustion of minerals or materials of manufacture; the likelihood of New Inventions, processes, or machines coming into use which may supersede and render Obsolete those whose value or depreciation are in question; or vicissitudes and catastrophes which cannot be provided for by ordinary Insurance. Conditions and contingencies such as these, if they are to be estimated and provided for, may be said to demand a Reserve or Sinking fund rather than a rate of depreciation, and in most cases it would be found desirable thus to isolate them in the accounts; but whatever be the precise method of doing it, they must be duly considered.

*See page* 18.

*See page* 20.

**Reserve fund.** *See page* 65.

**Tenure.**

In regard to Tenure, if the factory be only rented by the occupier, then the sum to be provided for depreciation will depend partly upon the conditions of tenancy; and if the rent covers fair wear and tear, the occupier need only keep the plant that belongs to the landlord in working order for his own purposes. As, for instance, in cases where a tenant possesses looms or other machines, while the landlord provides the workshop and engine-power, but leaves the current repairs to the tenant.

**Rent may cover depreciation.** *See page* 88.

**Factory built on leasehold land.**

A more usual tenure is that under which the premises are built by the occupier on land held on Lease, with the usual condition that the buildings and the permanent Fixtures become the property of the ground landlord at the end of the term. Without here going into the legal question of what constitutes landlord's fixtures, it may be said that in the case of fixtures added to a building for purposes of trade or manufacture the law leans more to the interests of the tenant than in the case of ordinary house fixtures. Where the circumstances would admit of doubt, proper stipulations in the agreement of tenancy should have been made. There are, however, few trades in which, if the tenant has equipped the factory with plant, all of it can be removed by him.

**Fixtures.** *See page* 118.

*See page* 96.

In the absence of a stipulation that the landlord must release, or pay for, such additions to the freehold, the provision of a Sinking Fund sufficient to give back the capital expended by the tenant becomes a matter of great importance. When the lease is for a long term, the annual charge or premium, if it begin with the lease, will not be found burdensome, and moreover the annual charge must not be considered as all due to the terminable tenure, because a freeholder would incur a considerable proportion of it—even if repairs be duly attended to—to compensate for the reduction in value due to time and use. In other words a depreciation rate would be necessary to compensate for wear and tear, and in the later years of a leasehold term, this would become merged in a sinking fund to repay all the capital.

**Sinking funds.**

*See* **Leasehold Assurance,** *page* 60.

**Not all due to tenure.**

But as under these conditions the tenant will fall under no obligation to give up more than the terms of his lease compel, he will, while maintaining the plant to the end of the term in sufficient order for his own purposes, abstain from replacing obsolete fixtures by new ones, and in regard to portions which are seldom used, may even let them wear out before the lease ends. Even if the occupier is to deliver up the factory in good tenantable condition, it does not follow that the repairs shall have been effected with so liberal a view to the future as the occupier might have as owner; nor is it to be assumed that fixtures fairly worn out in the work of the factory should be replaced by new ones. Therefore, as against his sinking fund, the occupier will, in the last years of his term, reduce the cost of maintenance.

**Tenant's renewals limited.**

**Maintenance in later years of lease.**

The Permanence or steadiness of profitable employment or the reverse has to be taken into account in deciding on the depreciation in the value of plant. A factory may be employed in some subsidiary trade, or in supplying some other undertaking which is not certain of continuing; or a patent, or a privilege, or a contract for a term of years may

**Permanency of employment affects value.**

*See also page* 50.

be near its termination. Owing to contingencies of this sort, which are too various to enumerate, the conditions of past successful working may be liable to such serious alteration or actual termination, that it is obvious a high rate of depreciation should be written off the plant, so as to bring down its nominal value to that which it will have under any such anticipated contingency. In the case of terminable undertakings an ordinary depreciation rate should really be supplemented by a Sinking fund, so that the capital sunk in the plant may be recovered.

*See page* 50.

**Removal of plant.**

*See page* 60.

*See also page* 52.

**Fluctuation in trade.**

There are manufactures which, though they may be fairly considered permanent, are subject to violent Fluctuations, rendering plant idle for considerable periods. Such are the lace trade, and others depending on fashion. In calculating the cost of manufacture and the profit obtainable in trades such as these, a higher rate of depreciation should be assumed in years when the plant is in full operation, to make up for idle years when little or no profits are earned; for though the actual wear and tear during these idle years may be small, the liability to deterioration and waste always continues.

*See page* 39.

**Plant may become obsolete.**

Again, the possibility of New Inventions, processes, or machines coming into use, which may supersede or render obsolete an existing plant, is a contingency that presses on many manufacturing trades, and especially on those which are of a new kind or in a transition state. This risk, which may be said always to exist to a certain extent, is one of degree, and in some trades it is the greatest risk of all. In some factories there is little risk of machinery becoming obsolete; in others the risk is confined to certain parts of the plant. Thus, in an engineering factory, although steam engines, steam hammers, lathes, and other machines of a customary kind are subject to improvement, and may for particular purposes be superseded, they are of use in so many kindred trades that they have a value till worn out,

**Customary plant always valuable**

*See page* 96.

even if at worst they have to be sold to other users. So also in a hosiery factory there are certain machines which have been proved by a long experience to be always required, while other of the machines may be liable to become obsolete. Invention is constantly being directed to automatic processes which may perform easily and mechanically what has hitherto been possible only with highly skilled labour or superintendence; and where radical alterations and improvements are being made from time to time in plant of a special kind, most of it useless for any other purpose, it would be unsafe to write off for depreciation the mere loss by wear and tear unless the rate on such a basis reduced the book value rapidly.

**Depreciation of obsolete plant.**

New Inventions are generally directed towards a Saving in Labour and an Improvement in the product, and special plant, when once superseded by such inventions, may prove unsaleable as second-hand plant, except in so far as it may have a piecemeal or scrap value, because no reduction in price of the superseded machinery would balance the expenditure in labour its use would involve, or the inferiority of its productions. The risk may arise, not from improvements in the machinery, but from alterations in the kind of product, rendering new machines necessary to suit new patterns or types. Contingencies such as these should encourage an ample reduction of nominal value in the early years of working, so as to bring down the book value of the plant to a point which will allow even of dismantling without serious loss. In such trades, profits should be large enough to allow for a liberal and rapid writing off of capital value. The same security is attained by the constant addition of new and improved machinery out of revenue; and undertakings in which the profits of prosperous times have been applied in this way in the renewal of plant rather than in the distribution of high dividends, have a considerable advantage, when trade be-

**Obsolete plant unsaleable.**

*See page* 95.

**Nominal value should be reduced,**

**or maintained by additions.**

comes dull, in competing with rival undertakings burdened with an unrelieved capital account.

**Special risks needing insurance.**

In certain trades there are other contingencies to be provided for before the net earnings can be fairly treated as profit, and though they do not strictly come within the scope of a depreciation rate, they may be referred to here. Such are risks which demand an insurance fund, but to which the ordinary systems of insurance are inapplicable. For instance, in or about a mine or quarry, there may be a risk of flooding, which would render useless the machinery and plant; or in a factory where highly inflammable or explosive articles are made, the risks may be so great or uncertain that no insurance company will underwrite them at any reasonable rate.

**Reserve fund separate from depreciation.**

But while as between a few partners it might be convenient to consider all these circumstances as part of one general system of depreciation, they would, in the case of numerous partners, or of a joint-stock company, be more properly provided for by a Reserve fund, stated in the accounts, and distinct from the depreciation by wear and tear. For, as it is impossible, by a mere annual writing off, to exactly balance uncertain contingencies, the grouping of all together may tell unfairly in either direction on the holding of those who have only a fleeting interest in the undertaking, or who cannot afford to stand by their investment to a future day.

**Accounts made clear to sleeping partners.**

To those who are concerned in the management, and who know the basis on which a general rate has been arrived at, the name by which the provision is stated may be a matter of indifference; but to partners or shareholders who are unaware of the circumstances, a separate reserve fund will ensure a fairer valuation of their property; and in case of a change or termination of the partnership, or of a cessation of the business, there is then a specific fund in hand which may even render a valution unnecessary. But those who are responsible for the management sometimes prefer to include in the depreciation rate what is really a reserve or insurance fund, so as to disguise the economies they are practising, and avoid the claims of shareholders who might prefer to divide and appropriate an undiminished income.

**Economies disguised by managers.**

On the other hand, it is sometimes the case that instead of actually writing down the value of machinery and plant, the full value is retained in the books of account, but a separate fund entitled "Depreciation and Reserve" is established by the application of part of the profits. The association of these two matters is however inadvisable, as shareholders may be led to believe that there is an actual fund at their disposal when the book entry really represents the loss by what is worn out or obsolete.

**Depreciation and reserve should be separate.**

In regard to Reserve funds, the question sometimes arises whether the money so set apart may properly be employed in the business itself, or whether it should be invested outside the business. If the object of the reserve be to provide ready money for some sudden call, the latter plan may be expedient, but in a manufacturing business the reserve may generally be best employed in it. Money can seldom be safely invested so as to be immediately available and yet at a rate of interest as high as that which a manufacturer could afford to pay for the use of it. If some of the capital employed in the factory is borrowed, such a use of the reserve fund will go to diminish the need for borrowing.

**Investment of reserve funds**

**in the business itself.**

The current of events may be the reverse to those just supposed. Thus, the value of the site on which the factory stands may be increasing in value by the growth of the town and neighbourhood, or the demand for the products of the factory may be increasing at a greater rate than the competitive supply, or the reputation of the factory may be increasing its trade and profit. But circumstances such

**Increasing value of the site.**

*See page* 83.

as these, however much they may increase the real value of the undertaking and may justify a corresponding valuation in the case of change in partnership or sale of shares, cannot safely be set against actual physical deterioration of the plant. The latter, as a distinct and unavoidable circumstance, should be dealt with on its merits, and improvements in another direction be left to a subsequent valuation, when the real maximum value has to be ascertained.

**Deterioration of plant still continues.**

*See page* 82.

In a joint-stock company effect may be given to such assumed increase in value by the higher market value of the shares; further, the original capital of a company may be increased under such circumstances by the distribution to the shareholders of new shares as "stock dividend."

**Stock dividends.**

*See page* 45.

## CHAPTER II.

### DIVISION INTO CLASSES FOR DEPRECIATION.

**Valuation as a basis for depreciation.**

IN order to estimate correctly the alteration in value which the capital sunk in factory plant undergoes from year to year, it is necessary to have some record of the original value or cost as a starting point. If the factory has been bought, the price forms this basis; if it has been built and equipped by the occupiers, there will either be a record of capital expenditure, or if not, as frequently happens in factories which have grown up by slow and irregular additions, and it be desired to inaugurate a proper system, a valuation will be necessary, to which subsequent depreciation rates can be applied. It may be that each annual review will show a growth of value by mere extension, even after deducting for deterioration; but it is important to take strict account of the latter, so as not to allow the nominal capital to be unduly swelled.

*See page* 56.

**Prescribed rates of depreciation.**

In some undertakings, not only the method, but the rate of depreciation is fixed in the deed of partnership or articles of association. It may have been a wise precaution to agree upon the principle of writing off, and even to fix a minimum rate, but it is obviously impossible to thus decide in advance on an absolute rate. Sometimes it is prescribed that deterioration by time and use shall be met by applying a fixed proportion of the profits to make good what has been lost. This method is more frequently adopted in the articles of joint-stock undertakings in France than in England; but it is obviously

**Fixed proportion of profits written off.**

unsound, as deterioration goes on even if no profits are being made. A percentage on the output or cost value of the products would be a better plan, and by referring to the accounts of preceding years a fair rate from this point of view may be established. While, however, this is useful, and indeed necessary, in estimating the cost of future production, it is not the best for dealing with the past. A percentage on the capital value as it was left at a previous review is for this purpose the most suitable. The sound plan is to write off this percentage in every year, besides charging to revenue the expenditure for repairs. It is, however, quite proper, in determining the rates of writing off for any year, to take into account the activity or slackness of certain departments. Credit has also to be taken in the plant account for actual renewals and additions which have been made.

**Writing off in proportion to output.**

*See page* 55.

**Repairs charged to revenue.**

*See page* 57.

It must always be remembered that to depreciate plant is to provide for contingencies as well as for the rate of wearing out which may be immediately visible. Therefore till a factory has been working for many years, any rate of depreciation must be tentative and subject to occasional adjustment. If a very low rate be adopted and yet after a course of years be shown to have been sufficient, it does not follow that the original adoption of such a rate was prudent. The risks have been run, and should have been provided for.

**Rates subject to adjustment.**

The great diversity of system renders a comparison between the practice in different factories difficult. In one, the greatest attention will be paid to repairs; renewals and even extensions will be effected out of revenue, and little or nothing written off for depreciation. In another, there may be apparently an ample provision made in the capital account for depreciation; but repairs may be neglected and a too liberal addition may be made to capital for so-called new plant.

**Comparison of factories difficult.**

To facilitate a correct estimate of deterioration it is expedient in many undertakings to divide the property into classes and to deal separately with each. Sometimes it is preferred to write off at one average rate from the whole of the sunk capital; and, if this average happens to be a fair one, the method has the advantage of simplicity. But simplicity is its only merit, and it has many drawbacks. Buildings and machinery generally require very different rates; and although a fair average may have been established, this is liable to be affected by the vicissitudes of particular years, and without modification may lead to considerable error. For instance, the manufacturing work of one year or a series of years, may have told more severely on certain parts of the plant or buildings than on other parts, and if the wear and tear due to such work have not been sufficiently noted, estimates for future operations of a similar kind, which allow only for the previous depreciation rate, may prove erroneous.

**Division of plant into classes.**

**Average rates liable to error.**

**Wear and tear not duly allotted**

There are frequent instances of factories engaged in multifarious operations, where a certain total result of profit is obtained, concerning which little or no investigation is made to ascertain to which branch of manufacture it is due. And in the absence of a proper analysis, the most remunerative class of operations may be neglected, or contracts taken in other branches at prices which would show a loss if the deterioration of plant due to them were properly allotted. As a corollary to the foregoing, it should be held dangerous to establish an average rate merely because it has been found appropriate in some other factory apparently similar, unless the conditions are exactly alike.

**Analysis of profit and charges.**

Sometimes an equal instalment from the original value of the plant is written off every year; sometimes each machine or item of plant is considered separately; but it is more usual to write off a percentage, not of the original value, but from the balance of the plant account of the

**Equal instalments of original cost written off.**

preceding year. Thus, if at the end of the first year 10 per cent. has been written off £100, then the 10 per cent. will in the second year be written off £90, and so on. Additions made within the year go, however, to neutralise such reductions, and in many cases to increase the actual total capital value.

*See page* 63.

**Division into classes.**

When dividing into classes the capital sunk in manufacturing plant, it is desirable, on the one hand, to have various distinct general categories; on the other hand, a minute subdivision is generally impracticable and inconvenient.

**Example of classification.**

The following is an example of the classification frequently adopted in factories:—Preliminary expenses; Land, including adaptation; Buildings and wharfs; Fixed plant and machinery; Steam engines, boilers and furnaces; Small loose plant and tools; Horses. To these must be added undertakings which are of a terminable or wasting kind, and for which special depreciation is necessary.

*See page* 50.

**Preliminary expenses show no available asset, should be quickly cancelled.**

*See page* 56.

In establishing a new manufactory there is often an outlay of capital for Preliminary Expenses, giving no actual asset in buildings, plant, or other tangible property. Such are the legal expenses connected with the formation of a joint-stock company, and in some cases there are the expenses of obtaining an Act of Parliament. Outlay of this kind may be just as necessary to the purpose in view as any other part of the expenditure, and may have been foreseen and reckoned on as part of the required capital. While, however, the earnings of the factory may, so long as they continue, afford a profit on such accessory outlay, the latter may be quite valueless as an asset in the event of the undertaking being wound up or sold, and therefore it is generally deemed prudent to cancel quickly this portion of the capital by writing it off annually out of the earlier earnings.

Railways, as already referred to, afford a conspicuous

exception to what is customary in private undertakings. In Great Britain very large expenses are incurred before anything is spent in actual works. Preliminary surveys, costly Parliamentary procedure, high prices for land, and compensation for supposed injury by severance or otherwise, have added greatly to the cost of railways and yet have added nothing to their earning power. Rates of carriage may be imposed which will afford interest on such preliminary expenditure, but if competition arises with some future line unburdened by these heavy charges, the earlier company may be compelled to lower their rates to the level of the rival concern. Although investors in railway shares seldom take care to distinguish the different purposes to which the capital outlay has been applied, or to value the available assets, and consider only the annual return they may expect on their shares, still an excessive capital may involve future risk as above explained. Each shareholder has to insure for himself against such a contingency, and it is to be noted that the loss will fall primarily on the ordinary shareholder to the exclusion of those who have a preferential claim on the revenue. Not only has an original inflation of capital to be considered, but periodical additions to capital.

**Cost of Railway Bills.**

**Not written off.**

If the undertaking has been purchased as a going concern, and a specific sum paid for Goodwill, somewhat similar considerations will arise. No rule can be set down for a rate of depreciation for this purpose. If the amount is small, it may be wiped off at once out of the earnings of the first few years, or it may form a legitimate object to which to apply the surplus profits of a prosperous year. But there are often cases where it would be unfair, as between partners, to write off entirely out of present earnings an outlay which was necessary to the establishment of the business, and of which, therefore, future earnings might justly bear a share. There are also cases

**Cost of goodwill written off.**

**Goodwill a valuable asset.**

*See page* 84.

**Trade-mark.**

*See page* 85.

where the goodwill forms so real and important an asset that it would be erroneous to cancel it in the capital accounts. Such a case for instance occurs when the name, or trade-mark, or brand of a manufacturer has been so long or widely established as to ensure a regular or profitable flow of business. Or the goodwill may have grown out of what was originally a monopoly by patent.

**Expenses of land purchase.**

*See page* 20.

Where preliminary expenses have been incidental to the purchase of Land which has since undoubtedly risen in value, such an increment may be held to sufficiently balance the expenses, which may then need no other consideration, as a sale at any future time would recoup the original outlay. So long, however, as the facts are correctly recorded in the books—so that in the case of a change in partnership or sale of shares the reduction which has been made in the burden of capital, and the enhanced value of the shares, will not be lost sight of—the writing off of all preliminary expenses is a distinct advantage.

## CHAPTER III.

### LAND AND BUILDINGS.

LAND occupied by a manufactory generally maintains its full value, and no provision for depreciation is necessary. In England, especially in large towns, the tendency is towards a growth in value ; the factory itself may have become the centre of an industrial population engaged in kindred and contributory trades, while the construction of railways, docks, and other facilities for transport may largely increase the value of the site. More than this, the expenditure for clearing and preparation of the site, as well as the formation of roads and wharfs, may have added a more than corresponding value to the land. **Land maintains its value, especially in large towns.**

Where a factory originally built in an open neighbourhood has been long established, it may have become so surrounded by a growing town as to have acquired value as a site for other classes of buildings entirely disproportioned to its original purpose ; and in large cities it constantly occurs that a factory may be dismantled, and the site sold for a price high enough to pay for the building of a larger and better factory elsewhere, on a more commodious site. **Site may become too valuable for factory.** *See pages* 78, 83.

While, however, it may be equitable in the case of a change of partners or business to revalue the site, or take into account its prospective value, the possible increment should not be mixed up with the annual accounts of the undertaking farther than to justify the maintaining the capital value of the land itself without **Revaluation of site.**

**Value of land kept separate from plant.**

depreciation. If nothing be written off the value of plant, although obviously deteriorated, on the plea that the increased value of the land balances the loss, a profit thus shown is obviously not due to the manufacturing trade. A division of profits from this source may, however, be temporarily justified in a time of depression, to allow of a moderate interest on capital, but even in that case the facts should be shown in the accounts.

**Land may fall in value.** *See page* 83.

But although the land in towns tends to rise in value, there are occasionally cases where its value may depreciate. Thus, the growth of the town, or the opening out of railways and roads in a new direction, or a change in the locality of the trade, may leave the factory isolated or unfavourably placed. So, again, when a trade has prospered because of its contiguity to a certain port, a diversion *See page* 125. of imports or exports may diminish or destroy the trade of the factory. Again, where a particular industry has flourished because of favourable Customs duties either at home or abroad *See page* 126. an alteration in the tariff may entirely alter the course of trade.

**Factory dismantled and land sold.** *See page* 96.

Thus it might prove necessary, if the factory were to be sold, to dismantle it for a more appropriate purpose in order to restore the land to its natural value. Even while the manufactory is still a going concern, it might be prudent to write off something from the original value of the land, so as not to leave all the burden of the loss to those who might be proprietors at a time of change. Sometimes depreciation is necessary, not because of any real falling off in value, but because the land was bought in a time of inflated prices. *See page* 83. As a general rule, however, no depreciation rate is needed for the capital sunk in land and its adaptation. *See page* 56. *See page* 52. Leaseholds need special consideration.

Buildings may be considered to include all structural additions to the land, and therefore, not only workshops and offices, but wharfs, railways, and tramways, may for the present purpose be placed in one category. It very often happens that in the accounts of manufactories no allowance is made for deterioration of buildings, it being considered that if kept in proper repair they are permanent. The term of endurance depends primarily on the solidity and quality of the original work, and thereafter on the attention paid to repairs. But besides current repairs, there must also be partial renewals from time to time, at intervals far apart in the early years of the undertaking, but shorter as the factory grows older. This would tell heavily, and perhaps unfairly, on the interest of those who happened at the later period to be proprietors, unless some provision had been made by writing off some of the value in the early years.

**Deterioration of buildings.**

**Durability, how determined.**

**Necessity for writing off.**

An undue cheapness in construction shows itself after a few years of working; or an alteration in the trade of the factory to heavier work than that for which the buildings were designed, may tend to weaken and destroy them.

In reckoning the proper rate of depreciation for buildings of brick or stone, they may be divided broadly into two classes; as those subject only to ordinary deterioration from time and weather, and those which suffer also from abrasion, concussion, or other special incidents of working. In an engineer's factory, for instance, the pattern shops, fitting shops, lofty chimneys, storehouses, and offices might come in the first division; while the foundry, smithy, and, in some heavy trades, the machine shops and erecting shops might, as being liable to rougher usage, be placed in the second. And even in lighter trades, if quickly-running shafting or machinery be attached to the walls or roof framing, the effect on the building may be injurious.

**Wear and tear of buildings.**

**Rough usage of buildings.**

If proper attention be paid to the roof-covering as well as to the painting of ironwork and woodwork—the expenditure being all made out of revenue—a depreciation rate of

**Rate of writing off.** *See page* 63.

1¼ per cent. would suffice in the first class, so reducing each original £1000 to £686 in thirty years, and a rate of 4 per cent. might be appropriate for the second class, reducing every £1000 to £665 in ten years. If, then, at the end of these thirty and ten years respectively £200 be spent in a thorough renewal, this new expenditure might be properly added to the capital value, and the writing off for depreciation go on again. In most factories an average of 1½ per cent. for buildings will generally be found appropriate if due attention is paid to repairs. Such a rate will bring down a value of £1000 to £635 in thirty years.

**Amount written off applied to renewals.**

**Average rate for buildings.**

**Wood buildings.**

Buildings of wood or iron would require a higher rate, ranging from 4 to 10 per cent., according to the design and solidity of the buildings, the climate, the care and the regularity of the painting, and according, also, to the usage they are subjected to. Thus, strong wooden buildings in a cold dry climate might last almost as long as brick structures, while light wooden sheds in England would not last one-sixth as long. Strong well-fitted iron buildings will last as long as brickwork if properly painted, but the cheaper kind of iron buildings, on light columns, with loosely fitted roof framing and covered with corrugated iron, galvanised, but unpainted, would in a damp climate be so wasted by rust and shaken by the wind, that they would be quite worn out in from ten to twenty years, the old materials being then almost worthless.

**Iron buildings.**

**Wear and tear in ironworks.**

In factories where such operations as melting, hammering, and rolling of iron are carried on in buildings of the last-mentioned sort, a depreciation rate of 5 per cent. would be quite inadequate; and even substantial brick buildings subjected to the vibration due to steam hammers and the strains of heavily loaded cranes might require, even though current repairs were attended to, a rate of 5 per cent. to provide for occasional thorough renewals. In any case, the object in view in deciding upon the system and rate of depreciation should be to have always a book value not exceeding that which a fresh valuation would give; and periodical valuations may be required to show whether an increased or diminished rate was necessary for the future.

**Depreciation balanced by renewals.**

The question as to how far the expenditure on current repairs and renewals would alone meet the case, depends, as has already been stated, a good deal on the size or extent of the factory. Thus, in large and long-established works, a certain proportion of the whole might be renovated and even rebuilt every year, and this, if done out of revenue, might render a depreciation rate unnecessary. But in a small factory, or one recently established, such renewals might not become necessary for many years, and a depreciation rate, dividing the loss over many years, would be needed to accumulate a fund to be drawn upon in the future. The risk of error is greater when divided over many years than in those cases where the annual outlay shows clearly the fleeting value of the buildings.

*See page* 2.

*See page* 8.

Furnaces and ovens, which wholly or in part are actually destroyed by the operations of manufacture, may have to be rebuilt so often that if this be done out of revenue no depreciation may be necessary. But where they are too few to give an annual average of renewals, a special system of depreciation or a reserve fund is required.

**Wharfs and railways.**

Wharfs and railways should be maintained out of revenue, but unless they be of large extent, thus ensuring every year an average expenditure for renewals, a rate of depreciation will also be necessary, which will, in effect, serve as a reserve fund. For instance, if there be works of this kind having an original cost of £1000, a rate of 3 per cent. will in ten years reduce the book value to £737. If then £200 be expended on actual renewals, such as sleepers, rails, and masonry, this new outlay may be properly added to the book value, and the same rate of

*See page* 56.

depreciation be continued. Where the quantity of rails is sufficient to be classed as a separate item, it is generally considered prudent to write the value down to that of old iron or steel, and there leave it, the capital account being brought back to its original amount by future renewals. The circumstances which arise from a limited tenture, or in
*See pages* 51, 118. regard to fixtures as between landlord and tenant, are referred to elsewhere, and sometimes involve legal questions which need not be dealt with here.

# CHAPTER IV.

## PLANT AND MACHINERY.

FIXED plant and machinery are sometimes included in one category with buildings, and an average rate written off the whole. It is, however, the purpose here to consider them separately, and this is necessary even if an average rate is to be adopted.

**Plant kept separate from buildings.**

There is a wide range within which values may alter, but a proper estimate may be approached, and the issues narrowed, by regarding first the extreme limits of value. For instance, the highest value of any machine will be the cost of a similar machine, ready for immediate use, together with the expenses of installation. If invention and skill have been bestowed on any additions, a higher value may have been reached than is represented by the orginal cost and the subsequent outlay, and this notwithstanding that the machine is partly worn. The best proof of efficiency in a machine may be afforded by actual working. Such a proved value may be again increased by surrounding circumstances, such as that, as part of a going concern, profitable employment is assured, or that the readiness of the machine for immediate use gives it a value above that of a new machine, which would take time to get into working order. But these latter considerations, while demanding full weight in the case of valuation on a change of ownership, cannot properly affect a scheme of depreciation for wear and tear.

**Extreme limits of value.**

*See page* 97.

**The highest value.**

**Efficiency proved by working.**

*See page* 74.

The lowest extreme is represented by the "scrap" value,

**The lowest or scrap value.**

or the price which may be depended on for the old materials. The relation which this lowest value bears to the original cost obviously depends on the proportionate value of the materials and that of the labour that has been bestowed upon them. Articles of copper and brass may have a scrap value approaching nearly to the price when new. So also may articles of cheaper materials if of a simple kind. Thus, old rails, or railway chairs, may be worth as scrap iron half their original value. On the other hand, the scrap value of light and intricate machinery may be a mere fraction of the original cost. Again, the value of old material is sometimes greatly reduced by the cost of preparing it for re-use; such is the case with the removal and breaking up of cumbrous and heavy iron work.

**Valuable scrap.**

**Scrap expensive to utilise.**

Circumstances such as these must be taken into account, for the main factors in calculating a rate are—1. The Original value; 2. The probable working Life; 3. The Ultimate selling value when worn out or superseded. Therefore, in deciding upon an appropriate rate of depreciation which will in a term of years provide for the estimated loss, it is not the original value or cost which has to be so provided for, but that cost less the ultimate or scrap value.

**Depreciation rate, how based.**

With machinery, as with buildings, the first years of working show, in many cases, little or no reduction in value, and yet it is clear that, however long the working life is to be, it begins to shorten from the first, and the value must be depreciated accordingly. But this principle has to be applied with considerable qualification where repairs really renew the life of the machine and prolong greatly its period of useful work. For instance, a locomotive* during its life may have its wheel-tires renewed four times, its boiler three times, and be painted seven times, so that before the framework, the wheels

**Deterioration not apparent in first years.**

**Frequent renewals of same machine,**

**as in locomotives.**

* R. Price-Williams on "Rolling Stock." (See footnote, p. 3.)

and other more durable parts fail, and the engine is broken up, much more than its original cost will have been expended on it. The value of such renewals should be duly credited in a proper system of depreciation.

In the case of fixed machinery, worn out or superseded, it must always be borne in mind that the adoption of any new machine not only involves the cost of purchase, some of which could be recovered by an ultimate re-sale of it, but also the additional expense for installation; the latter outlay being irrecoverable, and only remunerative to the purchaser by the continuance of working.

**New machines involve cost of installation.**

The Deterioration of machinery depends on many circumstances, some of which relate to the Machine itself, and others to the mode of Using it. First, as to the machine itself, its quality, and the skill with which it has been set up affect its durability. In the case of a machine which has to withstand concussion or strains, the weight of the framework or other fixed parts must be sufficient to absorb the shocks of impact without undue vibration. Where the inertia of the framework is insufficient for this, oft-repeated strains will render the machine unsteady or untrue, and will destroy its efficiency long before it is in other respects worn out. The same unsteadiness may result if the machine is insecurely attached to its supports. In this respect velocity has to be considered as well as the force of the blows. A frame strong enough to absorb a certain strain may deteriorate if the strains are rapidly repeated. For slow speeds, an approximate balancing of the moving parts may suffice, while for high velocities, when the slightest inequalities are intensified by the speed, exact balancing and the most accurate fitting are necessary to prevent the machine or its supports being shaken loose and destroyed. If wearing parts have not been properly hardened, or if arrangements for making good the wear or

**Durability how determined.**

**Concussion and impact.**

**Effect of velocity.**

**Renewal of wearing parts.**

for inserting new parts have not been provided, the effective life of the machine may be limited to that of the wearing parts.

**Cleaning, painting, oiling.**

Care in management goes far to determine the durability of a machine. Protection from dirt or injury, periodical painting, and lubricating with good oil, may render one machine twice as durable as a similar one in which these precautions are neglected.

**Hours of work.**

**Effect of overtime.**

The hours of actual work have also to be considered in comparing the deterioration of one machine or factory with another. In some factories overtime is the constant practice, and the wear and tear correspond. This would be duly met if the reserve fund or depreciation rate were proportioned to the output; but under the usual plan of writing off annually a certain part of the capital value, the deterioration due to incessant working would not be provided for by a rate appropriate for ordinary working.

**Severity of working.**

**Undue straining**

**Piecework.**

**Precautions against over-working.**

Severity of working has to be taken into account as well as the hours of work. A certain margin of strength being given to a machine, there is a wide range within which it may be forced to its great detriment, without actual risk of accident. Thus, a steam boiler or engine may be worked with a higher pressure of steam than its designer intended, or toothed wheels be made to transmit greater power; or machines intended to deal with light materials, or to manufacture light goods, may be set to work on heavier materials and goods. Where production is stimulated by a system of piecework, the deterioration of the plant is likely to be more rapid than in a factory where the workmen are paid according to time only. Safeguards can be provided against excessive strains, yet when the labour of the workmen may be lightened, or their wages increased by forcing a machine, special care must be taken that the precautions are observed. Thus safety valves in boilers may be locked, registers of speed rendered inaccessible to the workmen, and other similar mechanical arrangements provided.

In very busy times, when there is a pressing demand for the products, and profits are large, it may be expedient and remunerative to work long hours, and to force the plant and machinery to their utmost power, even at the risk of a breakdown, so as to take full advantage of the transient high prices; but in such a case a corresponding rate would have to be written off for depreciation. **Forced working profitable.**

There is often in a factory some large or special machine which, though necessary to the execution of certain occasional work, is seldom used. The deterioration of such a machine is therefore slow, but as a machine seldom needed is not so saleable as one of an accustomed kind, it is best to include it in the general depreciation rate. **Machines seldom used.**

In small factories, where the purchase of new machines occurs but seldom, it is particularly important to provide for such outlay by an annual depreciation rate. In large factories, the purchase of new machines and the renovation of old ones are so frequent that the loss by deterioration is made manifest; the danger in these larger undertakings being that too much of the expenditure for renewals may be added to the capital value. If in an ironworks there be six steam hammers, it is probable that each year one of them may require extensive repairs, such as a new piston-rod, or cylinder, or anvil, while every second year a new hammer may have to be bought. Such outlay, if all defrayed out of revenue, might balance the average depreciation of the whole; but in a small factory, where only one steam hammer is employed, an annual depreciation rate would be required to balance the outlay when it comes. Discrimination is needed in allotting these charges, for, while it it prudent and necessary to provide for renewals by an accumulated fund, the expenditure when it comes may be fairly considered as tending to restore the capital **Depreciation in small factories** **less apparent than in large factories.** **Numerous machines afford an average.** **Value restored by renewals.** *See page* 57.

value. For a liberal rate of depreciation in preceding years will have brought down the book value of the plant to a point corresponding with its worn condition.

**Plant may become obsolete.** *See pages* 18, 95.

The risk of the plant becoming obsolete before it is worn out has already been referred to. Sometimes where a machine as a whole may continue serviceable, important parts may become obsolete. Thus, in an iron rolling-mill, new rolls may be cut to produce a certain pattern of bar iron, and if this pattern be of a standard shape and size constantly in demand, the rate of deterioration may be based on its probable durability and the number of tons of iron which the rolls will produce before they are worn out. If, however, the pattern be peculiar in shape or size, a higher rate of depreciation is necessary; indeed, it may be proper to charge the whole cost of the rolls to the first lot of bars produced. In this respect the rolls must be treated like foundry patterns, which are in some cases charged to one set of castings for which they have been specially made, and in other cases, as stock or standard patterns, are properly charged to capital. There are numerous other industries where a large proportion of the cost of manufacture is for the design and patterns, and a due depreciation in value is always of great importance.

**Design and size of product may vary, as in rolled iron, or foundry patterns.** *See page* 46.

**Systems of depreciation vary.**

In regard to the proper rate of depreciation for machinery, there is, even in well-managed factories of similar class, a wide divergence of practice. Thus, in a new factory doing a profitable business, private partners will, in their desire to be on the safe side, sometimes commence by writing off annually 10 per cent. from machinery of all kinds. Unless there be some apprehension of the plant becoming obsolete, this is generally too liberal a rate for fixed machines, unless it is neutralised in some other way. In other cases, the records of many years' working may show that 2½ per cent. is sufficient, because

**Low rate may prove sufficient.**

the machinery was good in kind and quality to begin with, partly also because the expenses of installation and of liberal repairs have been defrayed out of revenue, and partly because the machines have been moderately worked.

**Engineering factories.** In engineering factories the rate which will probably meet the deterioration will generally be found between 5 and 10 per cent. Where the work is of a moderate kind which does not strain the machines severely, and where the hours of working do not average more than sixty per week, 5 per cent. would generally suffice for machinery, cranes, and fixed plant of all kinds, if steam engines and boilers be excluded. **Average rates.** Where there is a diversity of machinery and plant, and the past accounts of twenty years to refer to, it is not difficult to arrive at an appropriate rate and to make periodical revisions.

**Repairs and renewals.** Repairs and renewals are sometimes of such a kind as to increase the value of plant, and nothing need be written off; while in other cases a very low rate will suffice. **Blast-furnaces.** For instance, in the case of blast-furnaces no deterioration may appear to take place for the first two or three years, and the expenses afterwards will be mainly those due to re-lining. As such expenses must obviously be defrayed out of revenue, a depreciation rate of 5 per cent. will generally prove sufficient, but it should take effect from the commencement, leaving any modification of the rate to be considered after a period of ten years. As the deterioration depends mainly on the severity of the working, a rate based upon the output rather than on the capital cost may be appropriate. **Rolling-mills.** Such a rate as 5 per cent. would be quite insufficient for the machinery of a rolling-mill, if that were the only provision for renewals. Even if a rate of 7½ per cent. be deemed appropriate for the first four years, a valuation at the end of that period may show that some rate between 10 and 20 per cent. will be necessary to meet effectually the depreciation in value due to wear and tear, and to the fact that the machinery is likely to become old-fashioned. But if, besides current repairs there are constant renewals and additions out of revenue, no writing down of the value may be necessary.

**Steam engines and boilers.**

Steam engines and Boilers, if classed separately from the other machinery of a factory, would generally require a higher rate of depreciation, and if again separated, boilers a higher rate than engines. Well-made, slowly-working engines engaged in regular work will, if properly maintained, occasionally last for fifty years. But in the great majority

**Wide variation of durability.**

of cases no such durability can be reckoned on. So wide is the possible variation, that special examinations of engines and boilers should be made at each annual balancing of accounts. If a well-made non-condensing stationary engine with Lancashire boiler, cost, including foundations,

**Rate for engines.**

£500, it would be prudent to write off $7\frac{1}{2}$ per cent. the first year, and $7\frac{1}{2}$ per cent. annually from the diminishing value,

**Repaired out of revenue.**

this being sufficient if the minor repairs and renewals, such as new brasses and fire-bars, be paid for out of revenue.

*See page* 63.

At the end of ten years the book value will stand at £229. If, then, the cylinder be re-bored, possibly a new piston supplied, and the boiler renewed by the insertion of a new

**Value partly restored.**

furnace, at a total cost of £80, this sum might be added to the capital value, the depreciation rate of $7\frac{1}{2}$ per cent. continuing for a further five years till the value is reduced to £209. A new boiler would probably then be required, costing £200, and the rate of $7\frac{1}{2}$ per cent. again go on on the renovated value of £409.

**Portable engines wear out rapidly.**

Portable engines with multitubular boilers are liable to rapid deterioration, and there is a wide range of difference in durability according to the treatment they are subjected to. Engines of this sort when used for temporary purposes can seldom be so well protected and managed as when permanently fixed in a clean well-ordered workshop. Thus an annual rate of from 10 to 15 per cent. would be necessary as a commencement. A rate of 15 per cent. would in five years reduce an original value of £300 to £133. If, then, £50 be spent on repairs, the book value might be increased to £183, and the 15 per cent. rate go on, so that at the end of another four years the value would be reduced to £96. If then patched up at an expense of £50, it might at a low pressure of steam last a few years longer.

**Repairs and renewals.**

**Durable engines.**

On the other hand there are cases where, for well-made, well-managed engines of this class, 10 per cent. would be ample, such a rate reducing £300 to £177 in five years. No exact rule can, however, be made for steam engines of this kind. The deterioration depends first on the size of the engine—small sizes wearing out quickest; on the care in firing and kind of fuel and water; on whether the working is forced; on the original quality of the engine and the care given to repairs; on the protection from dirt; and on the hours the engine is kept at work. In extreme cases a portable engine is quite worn out in five years, and its value to be broken up would be about one-twelfth part of its original price.

**Causes of wear in portable engines.**

**Contractors' locomotives.**

Contractors' locomotives working on imperfect railroads soon wear out, and a rate of 20 per cent. is generally required, bringing down the value of an engine costing £1000 to £328 in five years. Whatever be the exact rate adopted for steam engines, it should be estimated liberally for the first five years. Revision will then show if the rate needs alteration.

**Boilers and furnaces.**

In trades where steam engines, steam hammers, furnaces, and boilers, form a large proportion of the total plant, they should either be classed separately from the other machinery, or the rate appropriate to them should determine that for the whole. But in engineering factories, an inclusive average rate is generally adopted, which, as already stated, will generally be found between 5 and 10

**Average rate.** per cent.; but even from this average it is sometimes considered expedient to exclude certain things, such as patterns and foundry boxes, which may either be included in loose plant, presently to be referred to, or be classed separately.

*See page* 48.

Before, however, leaving this part of the subject, it may be repeated that the slower the deterioration, the greater the importance of establishing a proper system. Where the deterioration is rapid, as in boilers and furnaces, the need for renewals forces itself on the attention of users, and the justice of charging expenditure on this account to revenue is so obvious that any other plan, though it might be deemed merely delusive in the case of private firms, would in the case of joint-stock companies be rightly considered dishonest. Where, however, the deterioration of plant is slow, an insufficient rate of depreciation may by mere inadvertence go on for many years before the error becomes apparent; and the loss, when at last it is realised, too often falls upon the wrong shoulders.

**Rapid decay self-evident.**

**Slow decay unnoticed.**

There are cases where it is very difficult to apply exact rates of depreciation, and yet where the uncertainty which causes the difficulty increases the need for writing off. In the large industries such as iron, steel, and chemical works, the improved methods that are continually arising render necessary an outlay of a speculative nature for new experiments and plant, which if successful will render much of the old plant obsolete or of diminished value. A large annual return may alone justify the outlay, and such return cannot safely be treated as profit without a considerable reduction in capital value. Therefore while in average or normal years of working a moderate rate of depreciation may suffice for mere physical deterioration, advantage should be taken of prosperous years to write down liberally the book value of the plant. As a matter of

**Iron, steel and chemical works.**

**Liberal writing off in prosperous years.**

book-keeping this may be done as described on page 57, so rendering some of what appears as profit liquid as resumed capital; or it may be effected by extinguishing debentures or repaying loans. Or if shareholders are unwilling to regard as cancelled an outlay which as yet has shown no sign of unprofitableness, new shares (equal in amount to the cancelled debentures) may be created and distributed as a bonus or "Stock dividend." Such an increase in the nominal share capital is a sounder plan than that of dividing the profit among the shareholders in money and maintaining the debenture or loan indebtedness. But before creating such new capital it should be clearly ascertained that there are real and tangible assets to represent it. Even additions to buildings and plant, though they may apparently increase the earning power, will not justify the new shares unless it be clear that there is no reduction in the value or usefulness of old plant, which will neutralise the addition.

**Stock dividends.** *See page* 22.

**Should represent tangible assets.**

**Betterment.** *See page* 4.

There are cases where, without addition to plant, one or more years of large profits, and the assumption that such earnings will be maintained, have led to the creation of new shares. Many industrial undertakings have been burdened in succeeding years by such inflation of capital, and as a remedy the shares have had to be cancelled or rendered valuable by the application of profits to new works and plant instead of to dividend.

**Risks of inflating capital.**

Loose plant and Tools can seldom be satisfactorily treated in the accounts by the system just described for buildings and fixed plant. They wear out too quickly, and writing off a percentage annually is not a satisfactory method when the rate would exceed 20 per cent. There are two other methods available. One is to value the miscellaneous loose plant every year, and the other is to write off nothing, but to maintain and renew entirely out of revenue, revaluing occasionally, say every fifth year;

**Loose plant excluded from average rate.**

**Renewed out of revenue.**

or, as a third plan, part of the loose plant may be treated according to the first method, and part according to the second.

**Classification of loose plant.**

Such a system is carried out in some engineering factories by dividing the loose plant into classes somewhat as follows:—Foundry boxes; foundry Patterns; rapidly wearing plant, such as iron and steel Tools, belting, chains, ropes, portable forges, carts, wheelbarrows and ladders; Horses.

**Foundry boxes written down to value of pig iron.**

Taking these in their order, a list is kept of Foundry Boxes, and this is assisted by casting on each box the year in which it is made, and marking on each its weight. The value is, in some factories, at once taken at that of pig iron, but more often is written down to that level in a few years. Supposing one box has been made, weighing 1 ton, at a cost of £12, then, if it is of a shape or size not likely to be wanted again, all the cost—less that of the iron—should be charged to the first set of castings, and the box at once broken up. But if the box be considered useful enough to keep for future use, one-half or even less may be charged to the first castings, and the remainder treated as an addition to capital; but this remaining value should be written down in three years to pig-iron value.

**Example.**

**Old and new boxes averaged.**

Another and simpler plan is to value all the boxes, old and new alike, at 20*s.* per ton above pig-iron price—that is to say a moderate average price, and not that which may be current at the time, although of course the current price would need consideration in case of valuation for a change of ownership. This summary method does not apply to the elaborately fitted boxes specially prepared for the processes of machine moulding. Such boxes may be properly classed among machine tools, and depreciated accordingly, but at a liberal rate, as they wear out quickly.

*See page* 73.

**Machine moulding boxes.**

**Foundry patterns,**

Foundry patterns may be taken as a type of the patterns or designs necessary in so many trades, and involving much cost not easily dealt with in the books of account. As a safe general principle or starting point, every casting or set of castings should pay for its pattern; and where some exceptional or peculiar shape is to be made, with no immediate prospect of using the pattern again, this is necessary if loss is to be avoided. There is a natural reluctance to break up costly patterns, and an equal reluctance to treat them as valueless. The storing of them is often continued for many years without return, and ultimately the patterns are broken up for firewood or scrap-iron, as the case may be. Much depends on the nature of the trade, whether of a repetition or miscellaneous kind. It is often expedient in a repetition trade, where a succession of orders may be reckoned on, to spend much money on the patterns, which may have a value many times that of the castings made from them in the first year. Even, however, if durable iron patterns have been made, they often become obsolete before worn out, and therefore should be quickly depreciated.

**seldom of permanent value**

**Storing of patterns.**

*See page* 86.

**Expensive patterns.**

Toothed wheel and pulley patterns may be said to have a permanent value; but since the introduction of wheel-moulding machines it is much less common to store such patterns. Many expensive patterns, especially of an ornamental kind, have a value quite dormant, because they are unknown to purchasers; and it is for this reason that the publication of illustrated catalogues may give life to a stock of patterns otherwise useless. But while this may extend the time over which the cost is to be distributed, the value should generally be written down to one-tenth of the cost in ten years. If not used often they have little value; if used often they soon wear out.

**Wheel and pulley patterns.**

**Value increased by cataloguing.**

Engineers' drawings should be charged to the particular work for which they have been made, but there may be a permanent value to be considered in the case of valuation for a change of ownership.

**Engineers' drawings.**

**Patents and Copyright designs.**
*See page* 85.

Copyright designs or patterns protected by patent may, of course, have a special value; but, as between partners, this should be written off rapidly, as such rights last only a short time. In the case of a change of ownership a new valuation should be made. In this category should be included the engraving blocks used for catalogue illustrations.

**Loose plant valued at half cost.**

In regard to the miscellaneous and minor Loose Plant previously enumerated, if depreciated by an annual percentage rate, one of 50 per cent. might be necessary, which would be inexpedient. It is a simple and better plan to value all, old and new alike, at half their original cost; such a plan being assisted, in the case of tools, chains, and other articles of iron and steel, by weighing them.

**Occasional valuations.**

**Value of loose plant constantly renewed,**

**without writing off.**

Or a new valuation may be made at intervals of five years, credit being taken in the accounts for the last preceding valuation, on the assumption that if the loose plant be maintained entirely out of revenue, the aggregate value will never diminish. The tendency will indeed probably be upwards in the case of a growing factory; and the proportion which the annual capital account for fixed plant bears to previous years will afford the necessary check. If the fixed plant has increased notwithstanding an annual writing off, it is generally safe to assume that the loose plant is also growing in value. By this plan of writing off nothing from loose plant and adding nothing to the capital account for new purchases, the articles so treated may be regarded as consumable stores.

**Horses.**

Horses deteriorate more rapidly than the inanimate fixed plant of a factory, and need a special rate or system of depreciation, for it is obvious that contingencies have to be provided for which would not occur in the case of machinery. Assuming that sound, well-seasoned animals have been purchased, that they are well cared for, and that all veterinary expenses are charged to revenue, an annual depreciation rate of from 15 to 25 per cent. will be necessary to provide a fund for renewals. Between these wide limits, the exact rate will be found to depend on the conditions of working, principally on the kind of roads. On the paved streets of a city the deterioration will be more rapid than on macadamised roads, and especially if the horses have to trot on the paved streets. The experience of omnibus proprietors, tramway companies, and others, shows that the working life of a horse is from three to six years, according to the care paid to feeding, shoeing, stabling, and moderate working; while the easier conditions under which the carting work of a factory may be performed would allow a life to the horses of from five to ten years. Taking all risks into account, a liberal rate should be adopted till the experience of a course of years has shown whether a lower rate suffices, or whether a higher rate is necessary to maintain the original capital value by the purchase of new animals.

**Rates of depreciation.**

**Working life, how determined.**

Horses, like the loose plant just referred to, may in many cases be excluded with advantage from the general depreciation rate, and either the plan of an annual valuation be adopted, or that of maintaining the full value by purchasing new horses out of revenue. The latter plan is the simplest, and is safe if the horses are numerous enough to allow a fair average of annual expenditure. Cartage is generally an uncertain and unsatisfactory expense in connection with a manufacturing business, and the tendency in modern factories is to avoid the use of horses by constructing branch railways, by using hydraulic or other capstans for haulage, and in the factory itself by mechanical traction.

**Horses excluded from depreciation rate.**

**Cartage.**
*See page* 128.

## CHAPTER V.

### WRITING OFF THE DIMINISHING VALUE OF TERMINABLE UNDERTAKINGS.

REFERENCE has been made to the provisions which may become necessary to meet the decreasing or wasting value of a factory held for a term limited by lease or otherwise. There are undertakings which by their very nature have only a transient value, and where therefore everything that has been consumed or is irrecoverable at the end of the term must be written off out of revenue if the capital of the concern is to be preserved intact. Such for example are Collieries and other Mines; Concessions or Leases for terms of years; and Patents.

*See page* 12.

**Undertakings of transient value.**

In mines the limitation may be by the consumption of the minerals, or by the termination or lapsing of the right to get them. If the tenure is freehold and the minerals inexhaustible, or so abundant as to last for one hundred years, the contingency may be deemed too remote to require consideration, and no more needs be written off for a decreasing value of the outlay for opening out the mine, or for depreciated plant, than would be necessary in a factory belonging to the occupier. Sometimes a mine already equipped or in operation changes hands, and obviously if the minerals will only last for a limited number of years, it will be necessary for the new comer or purchaser who works the mine, in calculating the net profit for any year, to write off from the gross income a part of the purchase money in the proportion which the year or the tonnage of minerals annually consumed bears to the length of

**Exhaustion of mines.**

*See page* 13.

**Annual writing off.**

lease or total tonnage. A provision of this sort may be stated in the accounts in the form of a sinking fund rather than as depreciation.

The foregoing is a case where the price paid for a colliery or mine includes not only the prospective value of the minerals, but a previous outlay for developing the mine, and for work and plant transferred to the purchaser, most or all of which outlay may be irrecoverable at the end of the term. But more usually the works and the minerals are kept separate. A sum may be paid to the vendor for the former, and the minerals paid for by an annual rent or royalty. Or the whole is merged in the rent or royalty, and no sum is charged for entering on the property. A sinking fund is then unnecessary, except for the works or plant added by the new occupier; but the enhancement of rent to cover or recoup the vendor for his capital outlay illustrates the similar provision that must be made by the new occupier in the case where he has paid a sum of money as purchase or premium for coming in. In Great Britain when new collieries are opened out by the lessees, the latter have seldom to pay a sum of money down, but only an acreage or tonnage rent, in which is often merged a minimum or dead rent. The lessees have then to spend what is necessary to open out the mine. Sinking the shafts, making underground roads, erecting winding, hauling and pumping machinery, constructing wharfs and railways, are all properly charged in the first instance to capital, but when the coal face has once been fairly opened out, all afterwards should be defrayed out of revenue as part of the cost of getting. There are obviously exceptions to this rule, where new districts in the mine have to be opened out, or new developments made, with a view to an increased output or future profit, and the exact allotment between capital and revenue may depend also on the system of mining adopted.

**Rent or royalty.**

**Cost of sinking irrecoverable.**

The annual investment for establishing a sinking fund **Sinking funds.** may vary considerably, according as the expenditure has been charged to capital or revenue, and according to the term over which the provision is spread. As an example :—If £100,000 be expended in opening out a colliery, not only must the profit provide a renumerative interest on such a speculative outlay and on the subsequent expenditure, but should provide for the re-imbursement of the *See page* 13. capital at the end of the term. If the lease or term be for fifty years, or if the minerals are estimated to last that time at the intended rate of getting, then this period forms a basis for such a fund. The stronger or more heroic method would be to write down the capital at the rate of £2000 a year, in addition to any depreciation for wear and tear. But such a plan presses hardly on the earlier years, while diminishing the capital on which interest has to be paid in the later years. A more equitable plan is to establish a separate sinking fund, accumulating at compound interest. **Invested at compound interest** A sum of £1030 annually, invested at $2\frac{1}{2}$ per cent. will accumulate in fifty years to £100,000, or if invested at *See pages* 60, 65, 69. 3 per cent., £890 will suffice. If 5000 tons of coal per week be got for fifty weeks each year, one penny per ton set aside will amount annually to £1040. A provision of from a penny to two-pence per ton is not uncommon in actual *See page* 12. practice. Income tax will also have to be paid, as has already been explained. If the lessees, however, can reckon **Leases may be renewed.** on a renewed lease, or a new lease for adjacent minerals where the earlier expenditure can be utilised, the case is altered ; or even where entirely new shafts and machinery may be wanted, the sinking fund of the first lease may be applied to such expenditure, and the capital value revived for a new term. In other words, the new outlay may be provided out of past revenue.

While mines afford the most conspicuous instances of temporary or wasting values, other examples may be cited.

Thus the owners of smelting furnaces or factories, depending on a local supply of minerals, may, though having no direct share in the mines, find their property greatly reduced in value when the minerals are exhausted. Or saw-mills or charcoal furnaces may be rendered almost valueless when the forest which supplied the timber is exhausted.

**Concessions for public works.** Concessions for public works are often granted for terms of years, at the end of which the privileges and plant have to be surrendered at a price less than the original cost, or sometimes without any compensation. **Railways.** In some foreign countries monopolies for railways or municipal charters for gas, water or drainage works are granted on such terms. **Municipal concessions.** In Great Britain, concessions for tramways are granted for limited terms of years, at the expiration of which the local **Tramways for limited terms.** authorities have the option of requiring the removal of the tramway; or of purchasing it from the proprietors at a price which shall include no compensation for the loss of prospective profits, or for the compulsory nature of the transfer, *See page* 79. or for anything beyond the mere property itself. On such conditions the capital of the undertaking is hardly likely to be entirely restored, for the original outlay will have included an expenditure for preliminary expenses and for **Preliminary expenses.** *See page* 26. plant which has become partially worn out. Unless there has been a yearly depreciation which shall have provided for the cessation of the privileges as well as for the wear and tear of plant, loss will obviously result. Some system of sinking fund is the best means of meeting this contingency, **Sinking fund to restore capital.** *See page* 60. and the method and cost of doing so is described in the next Chapter.

Manufacturers who take out patents will prudently abstain from treating their supposed value as an addition to capital which will neutralise the need for a depreciation of plant. But if a valuation takes place in the case of a **Wasting value of patents.** dissolution of partnership or in selling the business, the patent may have a real value which will have to be paid for. But the purchaser should recognise the wasting nature of the investment in dealing with the question of depreciation. In recent years large sums have been paid for patents, and there are joint-stock companies who have no other asset. Although if the business has been well managed some permanent advantage should have accrued by goodwill or otherwise, the system of a sinking fund above referred to is applicable here also. Indeed a business may be so dependent on the monopoly afforded by a Patent as to be valueless when the monopoly has expired.

*See page* 85.

**Sinking funds not allowed.**

Although, in dealing with capital sunk in wasting properties as here described, it may be deemed prudent to establish a sinking fund, the setting apart of an annual sum is not necessarily a revenue charge. In the case of a company limited by shares the course adopted must not be contrary to the Articles. In some cases the proprietors of such undertakings as have been here referred to prefer to treat as divisible income the full earnings without reserving any portion as a sinking fund ; in short, treating the shares or income as a terminable annuity. Where each partner or shareholder is made fully aware of the circumstances, and is therefore in a position to protect himself by re-investing a portion of his income, such a plan has at any rate the merit of simplicity, and may be permissible; but in the case of sleeping partners or a large body of shareholders, the best plan is to establish a sinking fund for the common advantage. If the principle be acknowledged, there are various methods of applying it. Thus where there is borrowed money in the form of debentures, the paying off and cancelling a proportion annually may leave only a capital value for which there are equivalent realisable assets.

**Debentures cancelled.**

# CHAPTER VI.

## EXAMPLES AND TABLES.

**Depreciating by percentage rates explained by tables.**

THE method described in the preceding chapters, by which the original value of factory plant is depreciated by writing off annually a percentage from the capital amount as it appeared in the accounts of the preceding year, may be further explained by the following tables and examples :—

**Table I. explained**

Table I., on pp. 63 and 64, shows the effect of different rates of depreciation for any term up to 30 years, and also up to 100 years. The Diagram on p. 62 illustrates Table I., by showing graphically the effects of different percentage rates. The vertical lines show divisions of years; the horizontal lines show divisions of values. The curved lines will be seen to cross the divisions of years at points of value corresponding with those in Table I., and the alteration in the curve indicates the decremental reduction in value as the capital becomes less.

**Diagram on page 62 explained.**

**Examples of Table I.**

*Examples.*—What will be the depreciated value in 12 years at the rate of 7½ per cent. per annum of a machine whose original value is £475? In Table I. the 7½ per cent. column gives 0·392,374 as the depreciated value of 1 after 12 years, and this multiplied by 475 gives 186·377 or £186 7*s.* 8*d.* Again, what will be the depreciated value in 70 years of a building whose original value of £1550 is written off at the rate of 1¼ per cent. per annum? The 1¼ per cent. column gives 0·414,569 as the value after 70 years, and this multiplied by 1550 gives 642·58, or £642 11*s.* 6*d.*

These examples, while illustrating the effects of different rates of depreciation, do not show what generally takes place, for renewals and additions may go far to balance the depreciation, and in the case of an increasing business may more than neutralise it.

**Example of depreciation in 30 years.**

To illustrate this more clearly, an Example is given of the alterations in the value of a factory during a course of 30 years, where, owing to the nature of the trade, the buildings are depreciated at the rate of 1½ per cent. per annum, and the plant at 5 per cent. Credit is taken for renewals and additions, but not for current repairs. The altering values are shown graphically on the Frontispiece Diagram, and are as follows:—

**Frontispiece Diagram explained.**

The vertical lines in the diagram show divisions of years, the horizontal lines divisions of £100 and £1000 respectively. The factory is constructed at a cost of £21,000, exclusive of loose plant. Of this sum, legal and other preliminary expenses have cost £400, which is written off in four equal instalments, as shown by the diagonal black line at the left corner of the diagram. Land to the value of £1900 is purchased, but a portion of it, being not at first required, is let off to a tenant, and £700 is expended in adapting the remainder by levelling, draining, fencing and paving it, thus making a total under this head of £2600. As shown by the thick black line, the value is not depreciated, but in the 14th year the portion let off is taken in, and £150 spent on its adaptation, raising the capital value in the books of account to £2750.

**Preliminary expenses.**

**Land.**

*See page* 29.

**Buildings,**

*See page* 30.

**depreciated and added to.**

The Buildings cost £10,000 and are depreciated at the rate of 1½ per cent. per annum, the diminishing value being indicated by the thick red line. If the renovations and additions be left out of the account, the depreciation would continue as shown by the dotted red line, which at the end of 30 years reaches a reduced value of £6354. But, as shown by the upper or rectangular red line, £320 is spent on additions in the 5th year, and as this sum more than balances the depreciation of that year, the mean, or real value, as shown by the thick red line, rises in that year; but the depreciation rate of 1½ per cent. being applied to this increased value, it again declines. During the 12th year an expenditure of £350 is made for structural renewals, and this is added to the capital account. During the 15th year, additional workshops are built at a cost of £1200, and again in the 25th year £600 is spent. At the end of 30 years the total expenditure on buildings, including the original outlay, but exclusive of current repairs, has been £12,470, and the capital value in the books of account stands at £8353.

**Renewals of buildings.**

**Additions.**

The Machinery and Plant, indicated in blue, show greater alterations. Only a sum of £8000 is spent at the commencement, space being left for additional plant. A rate of 5 per cent. is adopted, which if not neutralised by additions would depreciate the value, as shown by the dotted curved blue line, bringing the whole plant down to a second-hand and scrap value of £1717 in 30 years. But as shown by the upper or rectangular blue line, additions are made from the beginning, and continued, with the exception of a few years, throughout the whole term, the money being applied in three ways, *i. e.* to the renewal of worn-out or obsolete plant by purchasing new, the price obtained on resale of the old going to diminish the expense; to the renewal of important parts of old plant, or the enlarging of machines so as to add to their earning capacity; and lastly, to the purchase of additional plant, either to supersede manual operations or to extend the output of the factory.

**Depreciation of plant.**

**Effect in 30 years.**

**Expenditure, how applied.**

Expenditure under any of these heads may be justly added to the capital value, and therefore goes to neutralise the depreciation, and produces as the actual mean value the thick blue line, which shows by its undulations the upward effect of the additions and the continually depressing effect of the depreciation rate of 5 per cent. Thus, in the 2nd year £250 is spent; in the 3rd year £520; in the 4th year £120; in the 6th year £70; in the

**Depreciation neutralised**

**by expenditure.**

7th year £140; in the 8th year £450; in the 9th year £580; in the 10th year £680; in the 11th year £170; in the 12th year £50.

Trade has then become dull, and in the 13th year there is no expenditure on renewals. In the 14th year £200 is spent, and trade then reviving, and the business of the factory increasing, more land is taken in, and new workshops are built in the following year. In the 15th year £940 is spent on plant, and in the 16th year £1530.

**Plant increased.**

At the stock-taking at the end of the 16th year, after spending during 16 years £5700 in addition to the original outlay of £8000, the capital value in the books of account stands at £8084. Nothing is spent in the two next years. In the 19th year £150 is spent; in the 20th year £350; in the 21st year £400; in the 22nd year £400; in the 22rd year £500; in the 24th year £320; in the 25th year £600. In this year a new workshop is added, and in the 26th year £1060 is spent in plant; in the 27th year £510; in the 28th year £600; in the 29th year £450.

**Result in 16 years.**

**Further additions.**

At the end of the 30th year, the total expenditure from the commencement, including the original £8000, has been £19,040, while the value of the plant as depreciated appears in the books of account as £8073. There is the apparent anomaly that with a larger factory and an extended business the plant is worth no more than at first. The reduction is true as regards capital value, but the earning capacity is greater. That is to say, the factory and plant would be worth more to a tenant who paid rent, but who had not the burden of maintenance, while for the owner the plant would have a shorter life.

**Result in 30 years.**

**Capital value reduced, but rental value increased.**

Assuming that £8280, representing three-fourths of the expenditure during the 30 years, has been for the renewal of worn-out plant and the replacing of what has become obsolete, and that £2760, representing one-fourth, has been for extensions; then the new value of the plant left in

**Analysis of expenditure.**

working order at the end of 30 years would be £8000 + £2760 = £10,760, but taking the average remaining life of the plant—some of it being 30 years old, and some of it almost new—the amount of £8073 as appearing in the books of account would represent a present value.

If the 5 per cent. rate has been a proper one, this remaining value should be correct, as between partners, exclusive of any goodwill; and if the business of the factory be continued, an incoming partner should pay either directly for goodwill, or in a more liberal valuation of the plant, for the advantage of acquiring not only a fully equipped factory, but the profitable employment attached to it.

**Value with and without goodwill.**

*See page* 84.

The foregoing example shows the effect of depreciation rates maintained without alteration for 30 years, but in practice modifications might be necessary. Thus, the experience of the first 12 years might show that owing to the durability of the machines and their careful management, 5 per cent. was unnecessarily high, and that a lower annual reduction might suffice. On the other hand, the rapid wearing away of certain parts of the plant, such as steam boilers, might have shown that the average rate was insufficient; or, without such physical deterioration, a higher rate might be necessary to replace plant which had become obsolete.

**Rate of writing off modified.**

*See page* 42.
*See page* 18.

The deterioration of plant being as much an incident and expense of manufacture as the outlay for wages and material, though less direct and apparent, it is important thus to ascertain by occasional investigation what will be a safe but not excessive rate to allow for in calculating the cost of new operations.

Loose plant has not been included in the example just given. In a factory where depreciation rates of 1½ per cent. for buildings and 5 per cent. for fixed plant are

**Loose plant omitted.**

necessary, the loose plant would probably be of a kind needing frequent renewals, which it is better to treat as a current expense, writing off nothing from the capital value. *See page* 45.

**Table II. explained.**

Table II., on pp. 65 and 66, shows the accumulation of a Reserved fund with compound interest in a term of years.

**Example.**

*Example.*—What will an annual reserve of £250 amount to in 18 years with compound interest at the rate of 3½ per cent. per annum. In the 3½ per cent. column 24·5 is given as the accumulated value of 1 in 18 years. This multiplied by 250 gives £6125.

**Table III. explained.**

Table III., on pp. 67 and 68, shows how much must be invested annually as a Sinking fund to accumulate with compound interest to £1 in a given term of years.

**Example.**

*Example.*—How much must be invested annually at 4½ per cent. compound interest to accumulate to £1250 in 22 years? In the 4½ per cent. column 0·0275 is set against the period of 22 years, and this multiplied by 1250 gives 34·375 or £34 7*s.* 6*d.* as the sum to be annually invested.

**Compounding of interest not always practicable.**

While however Table III. shows theoretically the accumulation of sums invested annually at compound interest it is not always practicable to make the re-investment of small amounts necessary to obtain the advantage shown in the Table. To meet this difficulty some of the leading assurance companies have established a system of "Leasehold Assurance" by which in consideration of a fixed annual payment they are willing to take this responsibility off the hands of the investor. But assurance companies cannot safely allow such high rates as can often be obtained in private undertakings, where investments in debentures or otherwise may afford interest at the rate of 4 or 5 per cent.

**Leasehold Assurance.**

Table IV. explained.

Table IV., on p. 69, shows the rates of premium charged (1893) by the Atlas Assurance Company, and the rates of the other companies doing this kind of business are about the same. The premiums are given in the form of percentage rates on £100 and assuming that they are paid annually in advance it will be seen that they afford an investment at 3 per cent. compounded yearly. In case the insurer desires to withdraw his investment during the term of years, a liberal surrender value is allowed.

## DIAGRAM ILLUSTRATING TABLE I. (pp. 63 and 64).

### THE EFFECTS OF DEPRECIATION AT DIFFERENT RATES FOR TERMS OF YEARS.

*For Explanation, see page* 55.

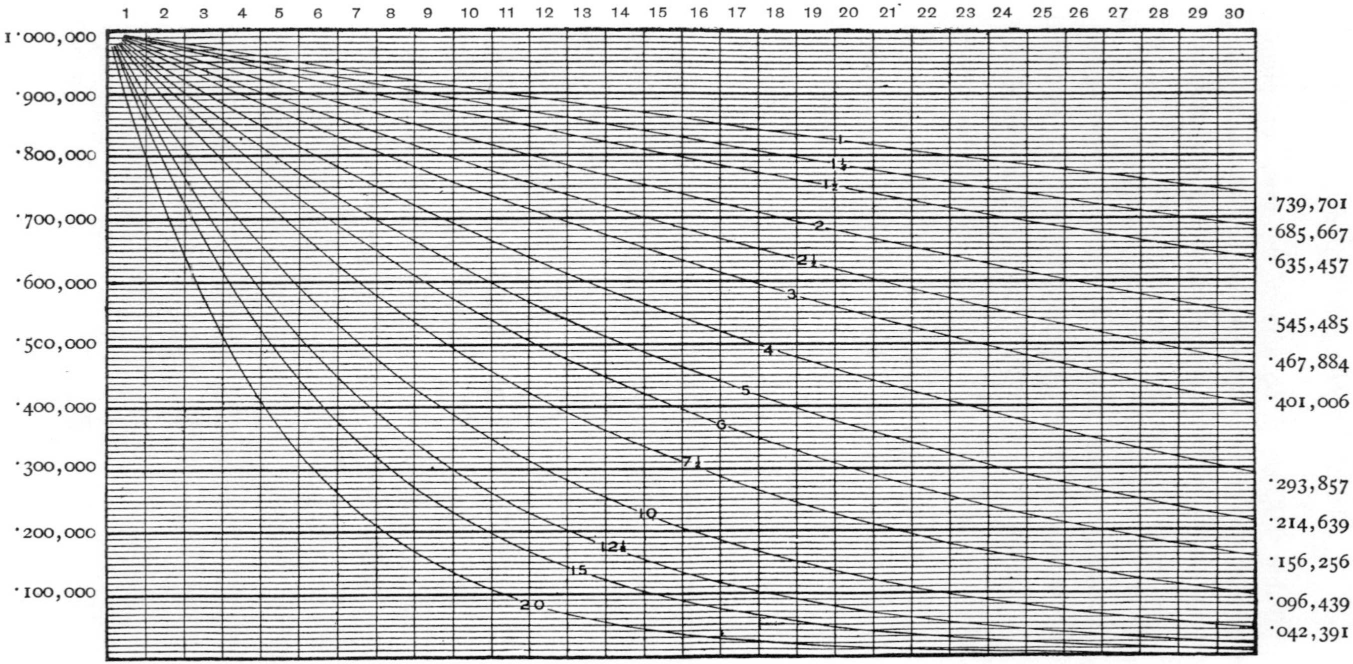

## TABLE I.

### The Effects of Depreciation at Different Rates for Terms of Years.

*For Explanation*, *see p.* 55.

| Years. | 1 per cent. | 1¼ per cent. | 1½ per cent. | 2 per cent. | 2½ per cent. | 3 per cent. | 4 per cent. |
|---|---|---|---|---|---|---|---|
| | 1·000,000 | 1·000,000 | 1·000,000 | 1·000,000 | 1·000,000 | 1·000,000 | 1·000,000 |
| 1 | 0·990,000 | 0·987,500 | 0·985,000 | 0·980,000 | 0·975,000 | 0·970,000 | 0·960,000 |
| 2 | ·980,100 | ·975,156 | ·970,225 | ·960,400 | ·950,625 | ·940,900 | ·921,600 |
| 3 | ·970,299 | ·962,967 | ·955,671 | ·941,192 | ·926,859 | ·912,673 | ·884,736 |
| 4 | ·960,596 | ·950,930 | ·941,336 | ·922,368 | ·903,688 | ·885,292 | ·849,346 |
| 5 | ·950,990 | ·939,043 | ·927,216 | ·903,921 | ·881,099 | ·858,734 | ·815,372 |
| 6 | ·941,480 | ·927,305 | ·913,308 | ·885,843 | ·859,068 | ·832,972 | ·782,757 |
| 7 | ·932,066 | ·915,714 | ·899,608 | ·868,126 | ·837,591 | ·807,982 | ·751,477 |
| 8 | ·922,745 | ·904,267 | ·886,114 | ·850,763 | ·816,652 | ·783,743 | ·721,389 |
| 9 | ·913,517 | ·892,964 | ·872,822 | ·833,748 | ·796,235 | ·760,231 | ·692,534 |
| 10 | ·904,382 | ·881,802 | ·859,730 | ·817,073 | ·776,329 | ·737,424 | ·664,832 |
| 11 | ·895,338 | ·870,779 | ·846,834 | ·800,732 | ·756,921 | ·715,301 | ·638,239 |
| 12 | ·886,385 | ·859,895 | ·834,131 | ·784,717 | ·737,998 | ·693,842 | ·612,709 |
| 13 | ·877,522 | ·849,146 | ·821,619 | ·769,023 | ·719,548 | ·673,026 | ·588,201 |
| 14 | ·868,746 | ·838,532 | ·809,295 | ·753,643 | ·701,559 | ·652,836 | ·564,673 |
| 15 | ·860,059 | ·828,050 | ·797,155 | ·738,570 | ·684,020 | ·633,250 | ·542,086 |
| 16 | ·851,458 | ·817,699 | ·785,198 | ·723,798 | ·666,920 | ·614,253 | ·520,402 |
| 17 | ·842,943 | ·807,478 | ·773,420 | ·709,323 | ·650,247 | ·595,825 | ·499,586 |
| 18 | ·834,514 | ·797,385 | ·761,819 | ·695,136 | ·633,991 | ·577,950 | ·479,603 |
| 19 | ·826,169 | ·787,417 | ·750,391 | ·681,233 | ·618,141 | ·560,612 | ·460,419 |
| 20 | ·817,907 | ·777,574 | ·739,135 | ·667,609 | ·602,572 | ·543,794 | ·442,002 |
| 21 | ·809,728 | ·767,855 | ·728,048 | ·654,257 | ·587,620 | ·527,300 | ·424,322 |
| 22 | ·801,631 | ·758,257 | ·717,128 | ·641,171 | ·572,930 | ·511,655 | ·407,349 |
| 23 | ·793,615 | ·748,778 | ·706,371 | ·628,348 | ·558,606 | ·496,306 | ·391,055 |
| 24 | ·785,678 | ·739,419 | ·695,775 | ·615,781 | ·544,641 | ·481,416 | ·375,413 |
| 25 | ·777,822 | ·730,176 | ·685,338 | ·603,466 | ·531,025 | ·466,974 | ·360,396 |
| 26 | ·770,043 | ·721,049 | ·675,058 | ·591,396 | ·517,749 | ·452,965 | ·345,980 |
| 27 | ·762,343 | ·712,036 | ·664,932 | ·579,568 | ·504,806 | ·439,376 | ·332,141 |
| 28 | ·754,720 | ·703,135 | ·654,958 | ·567,977 | ·492,185 | ·426,194 | ·318,855 |
| 29 | ·747,172 | ·694,346 | ·645,134 | ·556,618 | ·479,881 | ·413,408 | ·306,101 |
| 30 | ·739,701 | ·685,667 | ·635,457 | ·545,485 | ·467,884 | ·401,006 | ·293,857 |
| 40 | ·668,972 | ·604,622 | ·546,321 | ·445,701 | ·363,232 | ·295,711 | ·195,366 |
| 50 | ·605,006 | ·533,157 | ·469,689 | ·364,171 | ·281,988 | ·218,065 | ·120,885 |
| 60 | ·547,157 | ·470,139 | ·403,805 | ·297,554 | ·218,915 | ·160,806 | ·086,352 |
| 70 | ·494,839 | ·414,569 | ·347,163 | ·243,124 | ·169,950 | ·118,582 | ·057,410 |
| 80 | ·447,524 | ·365,568 | ·298,467 | ·198,650 | ·131,937 | ·087,445 | ·038,168 |
| 90 | ·404,732 | ·322,358 | ·256,601 | ·162,311 | ·102,427 | ·064,484 | ·025,375 |
| 100 | ·366,033 | ·284,256 | ·220,607 | ·132,620 | ·079,517 | ·047,552 | ·016,870 |

TABLE I.—*continued.*

THE EFFECTS OF DEPRECIATION AT DIFFERENT RATES FOR TERMS OF YEARS.

*For Explanation, see p.* 55.

| Years. | 5 per cent. | 6 per cent. | 7½ per cent. | 10 per cent. | 12½ per cent. | 15 per cent. | 20 per cent. |
|---|---|---|---|---|---|---|---|
| | 1·000,000 | 1·000,000 | 1·000,000 | 1·000,000 | 1·000,000 | 1·000,000 | 1·000,000 |
| 1 | 0·950,000 | 0·940,000 | 0·925,000 | 0·900,000 | 0·875,000 | 0·850,000 | 0·800,000 |
| 2 | ·902,500 | ·883,600 | ·855,626 | ·810,000 | ·765,625 | ·722,500 | ·640,000 |
| 3 | ·857,375 | ·830,584 | ·791,453 | ·729,000 | ·669,922 | ·614,125 | ·512·000 |
| 4 | ·814,506 | ·780,749 | ·732,094 | ·656,100 | ·586,182 | ·522,006 | ·409,600 |
| 5 | ·773,781 | ·733,904 | ·677,187 | ·590,490 | ·512,909 | ·443,705 | ·327,680 |
| 6 | ·735,092 | ·689,870 | ·626,398 | ·531,441 | ·448,796 | ·377,149 | ·262,144 |
| 7 | ·698,337 | ·648,478 | ·579,418 | ·478,297 | ·392,696 | ·320,577 | ·209,715 |
| 8 | ·663,420 | ·609,569 | ·535,962 | ·430,467 | ·343,609 | ·272,490 | ·167,772 |
| 9 | ·630,249 | ·572,995 | ·495,764 | ·387,420 | ·300,658 | ·231,617 | ·134,218 |
| 10 | ·598,737 | ·538·616 | ·458,582 | ·348,678 | ·263,076 | ·196,874 | ·107,372 |
| 11 | ·568,800 | ·506,299 | ·424,188 | ·313,811 | ·230,191 | ·167,343 | ·085,899 |
| 12 | ·540,360 | ·475,921 | ·392,374 | ·282,429 | ·201,418 | ·142,232 | ·068,720 |
| 13 | ·513,342 | ·447,366 | ·362,946 | ·254,186 | ·176,240 | ·120,905 | ·054,976 |
| 14 | ·487,675 | ·420,524 | ·335,725 | ·228,768 | ·154,210 | ·102,770 | ·043,981 |
| 15 | ·463,291 | ·395,292 | ·310,546 | ·205,891 | ·134,934 | ·087,354 | ·035,184 |
| 16 | ·440,127 | ·371,575 | ·287,255 | ·185,302 | ·118,067 | ·074,251 | ·028,148 |
| 17 | ·418,200 | ·349,281 | ·265,711 | ·166,772 | ·103,309 | ·063,113 | ·022,518 |
| 18 | ·397,214 | ·328,324 | ·245,782 | ·150,095 | ·090,395 | ·053,646 | ·018,014 |
| 19 | ·377,354 | ·308,624 | ·227,349 | ·135,085 | ·079,096 | ·045,599 | ·014,412 |
| 20 | ·358,486 | ·290,107 | ·210,297 | ·121,577 | ·069,209 | ·038,760 | ·011,529 |
| 21 | ·340,562 | ·272,701 | ·194,525 | ·109,419 | ·060,558 | ·032,946 | ·009,223 |
| 22 | ·323,533 | ·256,358 | ·179,936 | ·098,477 | ·052,988 | ·028,004 | ·007,379 |
| 23 | ·307,357 | ·240,958 | ·166,441 | ·088,629 | ·046,365 | ·023,803 | ·005,903 |
| 24 | ·291,989 | ·226,501 | ·153,957 | ·079,766 | ·040,569 | ·020,233 | ·004,722 |
| 25 | ·277,390 | ·212,911 | ·142,411 | ·071,790 | ·035,498 | ·017,198 | ·003,778 |
| 26 | ·263,520 | ·200,136 | ·131,730 | ·064,611 | ·031,061 | ·014,618 | ·003,022 |
| 27 | ·250,344 | ·188,128 | ·121,850 | ·058,150 | ·027,178 | ·012,425 | ·002,418 |
| 28 | ·237,827 | ·176,840 | ·112,711 | ·052,335 | ·023,781 | ·010,562 | ·001,934 |
| 29 | ·225,935 | ·166,230 | ·104,258 | ·047,101 | ·020,808 | ·008,977 | ·001,547 |
| 30 | ·214,639 | ·156,256 | ·096,439 | ·042,391 | ·018,207 | ·007,631 | ·001,238 |
| 40 | ·128,512 | ·084,162 | ·044,225 | ·014,781 | ·004,790 | ·001,502 | ·000,133 |
| 50 | ·076,945 | ·045,331 | ·020,281 | ·005,154 | ·001,260 | ·000,296 | ·000,014 |
| 60 | ·046,070 | ·024,416 | ·009,300 | ·001,797 | ·000,332 | ·000,058 | ·000,002 |
| 70 | ·027,584 | ·013,151 | ·004,265 | ·000,627 | ·000,087 | ·000,011 | .. |
| 80 | ·016,515 | ·007,083 | ·001,956 | ·000,218 | ·000,023 | ·000,002 | .. |
| 90 | ·009,888 | ·003,815 | ·000,897 | ·000,076 | ·000,006 | .. | .. |
| 100 | ·005,921 | ·002,055 | ·000,411 | ·000,027 | ·000,002 | .. | .. |

## TABLE II.

### Reserve Fund.—Accumulation of £1 per Annum with Compound Interest.

*For Explanation, see p.* 60.

| Years. | 2½ per cent. | 3 per cent. | 3½ per cent. | 4 per cent. | 4½ per cent. | 5 per cent. | 6 per cent. |
|---|---|---|---|---|---|---|---|
| 1 | 1·000 | 1·000 | 1·000 | 1·000 | 1·000 | 1·000 | 1·000 |
| 2 | 2·025 | 2·030 | 2·035 | 2·040 | 2·045 | 2·050 | 2·060 |
| 3 | 3·076 | 3·091 | 3·106 | 3·122 | 3·137 | 3·153 | 3·184 |
| 4 | 4·153 | 4·184 | 4·215 | 4.246 | 4·278 | 4·310 | 4·375 |
| 5 | 5·256 | 5·309 | 5·362 | 5·416 | 5·471 | 5·526 | 5·637 |
| 6 | 6·388 | 6·468 | 6·550 | 6·633 | 6·717 | 6·802 | 6·975 |
| 7 | 7·547 | 7·662 | 7·779 | 7·898 | 8·019 | 8·142 | 8·394 |
| 8 | 8·736 | 8·892 | 9·052 | 9·214 | 9·380 | 9·549 | 9·897 |
| 9 | 9·995 | 10·159 | 10·368 | 10·583 | 10·802 | 11·027 | 11·491 |
| 10 | 11·203 | 11·494 | 11·731 | 12·006 | 12·288 | 12·578 | 13·181 |
| 11 | 12·483 | 12·808 | 13·142 | 13·486 | 13·841 | 14·207 | 14·972 |
| 12 | 13·796 | 14·192 | 14·602 | 15·026 | 15·464 | 15·917 | 16·870 |
| 13 | 15·140 | 15·618 | 16·113 | 16·627 | 17·160 | 17·713 | 18·882 |
| 14 | 16·519 | 17·086 | 17·677 | 18·292 | 18·932 | 19·599 | 21·015 |
| 15 | 17·932 | 18·599 | 19·296 | 20·024 | 20·784 | 21·579 | 23·276 |
| 16 | 19·380 | 20·157 | 20·971 | 21·825 | 22·719 | 23·657 | 25·673 |
| 17 | 20·865 | 21·762 | 22·705 | 23·698 | 24·742 | 25·840 | 28·213 |
| 18 | 22·386 | 23·414 | 24·500 | 25·645 | 26·855 | 28·132 | 30·906 |
| 19 | 23·946 | 25·117 | 26·357 | 27·671 | 29·064 | 30·539 | 33·760 |
| 20 | 25·545 | 26·870 | 28·280 | 29·778 | 31·371 | 33·066 | 36·786 |
| 21 | 27·183 | 28·676 | 30·269 | 31·969 | 33·783 | 35·719 | 39·993 |
| 22 | 28·863 | 30·537 | 32·329 | 34·248 | 36·303 | 38·505 | 43·392 |
| 23 | 30·584 | 32·453 | 34·460 | 36·618 | 38·937 | 41·430 | 46·996 |
| 24 | 32·349 | 34·426 | 36·667 | 39·083 | 41·689 | 44·502 | 50·816 |
| 25 | 34·158 | 36·459 | 38·950 | 41·646 | 44·565 | 47·727 | 54·865 |
| 26 | 36·012 | 38·553 | 41·313 | 44·312 | 47·571 | 51·113 | 59·156 |
| 27 | 37·912 | 40·710 | 43·759 | 47·084 | 50·711 | 54·669 | 63·706 |
| 28 | 39·860 | 42·931 | 46·291 | 49·968 | 53·993 | 58·403 | 68·528 |
| 29 | 41·856 | 45·219 | 48·911 | 52·966 | 57·423 | 62·323 | 73·640 |
| 30 | 43·903 | 47·575 | 51·623 | 56·085 | 61·007 | 66·439 | 79·058 |
| 31 | 46·000 | 50·003 | 54·429 | 59·328 | 64·752 | 70·761 | 84·802 |
| 32 | 48·150 | 52·503 | 57·335 | 62·701 | 68·666 | 75·299 | 90·890 |
| 33 | 50·354 | 55·078 | 60·341 | 66·210 | 72·756 | 80·064 | 97·343 |
| 34 | 52·613 | 57·730 | 63·453 | 69·858 | 77·030 | 85·067 | 104·184 |
| 35 | 54·928 | 60·462 | 66·674 | 73·652 | 81·497 | 90·320 | 111·435 |
| 36 | 57·301 | 63·276 | 70·008 | 77·598 | 86·164 | 95·836 | 119·121 |
| 37 | 59·734 | 66·174 | 73·458 | 81·702 | 91·041 | 101·628 | 127·268 |
| 38 | 62·227 | 69·159 | 77·029 | 85·970 | 96·138 | 107·710 | 135·904 |
| 39 | 64·783 | 72·234 | 80·725 | 90·409 | 101·464 | 114·095 | 145·058 |
| 40 | 67·403 | 75·401 | 84·550 | 95·026 | 107·030 | 120·800 | 154·762 |
| 41 | 70·088 | 78·663 | 88·510 | 99·827 | 112·847 | 127·840 | 165·048 |
| 42 | 72·840 | 82·023 | 92·607 | 104·820 | 118·925 | 135·232 | 175·951 |
| 43 | 75·661 | 85·484 | 96·849 | 110·012 | 125·276 | 142·993 | 187·508 |
| 44 | 78·552 | 89·048 | 101·238 | 115·413 | 131·914 | 151·143 | 199·758 |
| 45 | 81·556 | 92·720 | 105·782 | 121·029 | 138·850 | 159·700 | 212·744 |
| 46 | 84·554 | 96·501 | 110·484 | 126·871 | 146·098 | 168·685 | 226·508 |
| 47 | 87·668 | 100·297 | 115·351 | 132·945 | 153·673 | 178·119 | 241·099 |
| 48 | 90·860 | 104·408 | 120·388 | 139·263 | 161·588 | 188·025 | 256·565 |
| 49 | 94·131 | 108·541 | 125·602 | 145·834 | 169·859 | 198·427 | 272·958 |
| 50 | 97·484 | 112·797 | 130·988 | 152·667 | 178·503 | 209·348 | 290·336 |

## TABLE II.—*continued.*

### RESERVE FUND.—ACCUMULATION OF £1 PER ANNUM WITH COMPOUND INTEREST.

*For Explanation, see p.* 60

| Years. | 2½ per cent. | 3 per cent. | 3½ per cent. | 4 per cent. | 4½ per cent. | 5 per cent. | 6 per cent. |
|---|---|---|---|---|---|---|---|
| 51 | 100·921 | 117·181 | 136·583 | 159·774 | 187·536 | 220·815 | 308·756 |
| 52 | 104·444 | 121·696 | 142·363 | 167·165 | 196·975 | 232·856 | 328·281 |
| 53 | 108·056 | 126·347 | 148·346 | 174·851 | 206·839 | 245·499 | 348·978 |
| 54 | 111·757 | 131·137 | 154·538 | 182·845 | 217·146 | 258·774 | 370·917 |
| 55 | 115·551 | 136·072 | 160·947 | 191·159 | 227·918 | 272·713 | 394·172 |
| 56 | 119·440 | 141·154 | 167·580 | 199·806 | 239·174 | 287·348 | 418·822 |
| 57 | 123·426 | 146·388 | 174·445 | 208·798 | 250·937 | 302·716 | 444·952 |
| 58 | 127·511 | 151·780 | 181·551 | 218·150 | 263·299 | 318·851 | 472·649 |
| 59 | 151·699 | 157·333 | 188·905 | 227·876 | 276·075 | 335·794 | 502·008 |
| 60 | 135·992 | 163·055 | 196·517 | 237·991 | 289·498 | 353·584 | 533·128 |
| 61 | 140·391 | 168·945 | 204·395 | 248·510 | 303·525 | 372·263 | 566·116 |
| 62 | 144·901 | 175·013 | 212·549 | 259·451 | 318·184 | 391·876 | 601·083 |
| 63 | 149·524 | 183·264 | 220·988 | 270·829 | 333·502 | 412·470 | 638·148 |
| 64 | 154·262 | 187·702 | 229·723 | 282·662 | 349·510 | 434·093 | 677·437 |
| 65 | 159·118 | 194·333 | 238·763 | 294·968 | 366·238 | 456·798 | 719·083 |
| 66 | 164·096 | 201·163 | 248·120 | 307·767 | 383·719 | 480·638 | 763·228 |
| 67 | 169·199 | 208·198 | 257·804 | 321·078 | 401·986 | 505·670 | 810·022 |
| 68 | 174·429 | 215·444 | 267·827 | 334·921 | 421·075 | 531·953 | 859·623 |
| 69 | 179·789 | 222·907 | 278·201 | 349·318 | 441·024 | 559·551 | 912·200 |
| 70 | 185·284 | 280·594 | 288·938 | 364·290 | 461·870 | 588·529 | 967·932 |
| 71 | 190·916 | 238·512 | 300·051 | 379·862 | 483·654 | 618·955 | 1027·008 |
| 72 | 196·689 | 246·637 | 311·556 | 396·057 | 506·418 | 650·903 | 1089·629 |
| 73 | 202·606 | 255·067 | 323·457 | 412·899 | 530·207 | 684·448 | 1156·006 |
| 74 | 208·672 | 263·719 | 335·778 | 430·415 | 555·066 | 719·670 | 1226·367 |
| 75 | 214·888 | 272·631 | 348·530 | 448·631 | 581·044 | 756·654 | 1330·949 |
| 76 | 221·261 | 281·810 | 361·729 | 467·557 | 608·191 | 795·486 | 1380·006 |
| 77 | 227·792 | 291·264 | 375·389 | 487·280 | 636·560 | 836·261 | 1463·806 |
| 78 | 234·487 | 301·002 | 389·528 | 507·771 | 666·205 | 879·074 | 1552·634 |
| 79 | 241·349 | 311·032 | 404·161 | 529·082 | 697·184 | 924·027 | 1646·792 |
| 80 | 248·383 | 321·363 | 419·307 | 551·245 | 729·558 | 971·229 | 1746·600 |
| 81 | 255·592 | 332·004 | 434·983 | 574·295 | 763·388 | 1020·790 | 1852·396 |
| 82 | 262·982 | 342·964 | 451·207 | 598·267 | 798·740 | 1072·830 | 1964·540 |
| 83 | 270·557 | 354·253 | 467·999 | 623·197 | 835·684 | 1127·471 | 2083·412 |
| 84 | 278·321 | 365·881 | 485·379 | 649·125 | 874·289 | 1184·845 | 2209·417 |
| 85 | 286·279 | 377·857 | 503·367 | 676·090 | 914·632 | 1245·087 | 2342·980 |
| 86 | 294·436 | 390·193 | 521·985 | 704·134 | 956·791 | 1308·341 | 2484·561 |
| 87 | 302·796 | 402·898 | 541·255 | 733·299 | 1000·846 | 1374·758 | 2634·634 |
| 88 | 311·366 | 415·985 | 561·199 | 763·631 | 1046·884 | 1444·496 | 2793·712 |
| 89 | 320·150 | 429·465 | 581·841 | 795·176 | 1094·994 | 1517·721 | 2962·335 |
| 90 | 329·154 | 443·349 | 603·205 | 827·983 | 1145·269 | 1594·607 | 3141·075 |
| 91 | 338·383 | 457·649 | 625·317 | 862·103 | 1197·806 | 1675·338 | 3330·540 |
| 92 | 307·843 | 472·379 | 648·203 | 897·587 | 1252·707 | 1760·105 | 3531·372 |
| 93 | 357·539 | 487·550 | 671·890 | 934·490 | 1310·079 | 1849·110 | 3744·254 |
| 94 | 367·477 | 503·177 | 696·407 | 972·870 | 1370·033 | 1942·565 | 3969·910 |
| 95 | 377·664 | 519·272 | 721·781 | 1012·785 | 1432·684 | 2040·694 | 4209·104 |
| 96 | 388·106 | 535·850 | 748·043 | 1054·296 | 1498·155 | 2143·728 | 4462·651 |
| 97 | 398·808 | 552·926 | 775·225 | 1097·468 | 1566·572 | 2251·915 | 4731·410 |
| 98 | 409·799 | 570·513 | 803·358 | 1124·367 | 1638·068 | 2365·510 | 5016·294 |
| 99 | 421·023 | 588·629 | 832·475 | 1189·061 | 1712·781 | 2484·786 | 5318·272 |
| 100 | 432·549 | 607·288 | 862·612 | 1237·624 | 1790·856 | 2610·025 | 5638·368 |

## TABLE III.

### SINKING FUND.—ANNUAL INVESTMENT TO PRODUCE £1 IN A TERM OF YEARS.

*For Explanation, see p.* 60.

| Years. | 2½ per cent. | 3 per cent. | 3½ per cent. | 4 per cent. | 4½ per cent. | 5 per cent. | 6 per cent. |
|---|---|---|---|---|---|---|---|
| 1 | 1·0000 | 1·0000 | 1·0000 | 1·0000 | 1·0000 | 1·0000 | 1·0000 |
| 2 | 0·4938 | 0·4926 | 0·4914 | 0·4902 | 0·4890 | 0·4878 | 0·4854 |
| 3 | ·3251 | ·3225 | ·3219 | ·3203 | ·3188 | ·3172 | ·3141 |
| 4 | ·2408 | ·2390 | ·2373 | ·2355 | ·2337 | ·2320 | ·2286 |
| 5 | ·1902 | ·1884 | ·1865 | ·1846 | ·1828 | ·1810 | ·1774 |
| 6 | ·1565 | ·1546 | ·1527 | ·1508 | ·1489 | ·1470 | ·1434 |
| 7 | ·1325 | ·1305 | ·1285 | ·1266 | ·1247 | ·1228 | ·1191 |
| 8 | ·1145 | ·1125 | ·1105 | ·1085 | ·1066 | ·1047 | ·1010 |
| 9 | ·1005 | ·0984 | ·0964 | ·0945 | ·0926 | ·0907 | ·0870 |
| 10 | ·0893 | ·0872 | ·0852 | ·0833 | ·0814 | ·0795 | ·0759 |
| 11 | ·0801 | ·0781 | ·0761 | ·0742 | ·0723 | ·0704 | ·0668 |
| 12 | ·0725 | ·0705 | ·0685 | ·0666 | ·0647 | ·0628 | ·0593 |
| 13 | ·0660 | ·0640 | ·0621 | ·0601 | ·0583 | ·0565 | ·0530 |
| 14 | ·0605 | ·0585 | ·0566 | ·0547 | ·0528 | ·0510 | ·0476 |
| 15 | ·0558 | ·0538 | ·0518 | ·0492 | ·0481 | ·0463 | ·0430 |
| 16 | ·0516 | ·0496 | ·0477 | ·0458 | ·0440 | ·0423 | ·0390 |
| 17 | ·0479 | ·0460 | ·0440 | ·0422 | ·0404 | ·0387 | ·0354 |
| 18 | ·0447 | ·0427 | ·0408 | ·0390 | ·0372 | ·0355 | ·0324 |
| 19 | ·0418 | ·0398 | ·0379 | ·0361 | ·0344 | ·0327 | ·0296 |
| 20 | ·0391 | ·0372 | ·0354 | ·0336 | ·0319 | ·0302 | ·0272 |
| 21 | ·0368 | ·0349 | ·0330 | ·0313 | ·0296 | ·0280 | ·0250 |
| 22 | ·0346 | ·0327 | ·0309 | ·0292 | ·0275 | ·0260 | ·0230 |
| 23 | ·0327 | ·0308 | ·0290 | ·0273 | ·0257 | ·0241 | ·0213 |
| 24 | ·0309 | ·0290 | ·0273 | ·0256 | ·0240 | ·0225 | ·0197 |
| 25 | ·0293 | ·0274 | ·0257 | ·0240 | ·0224 | ·0210 | ·0182 |
| 26 | ·0278 | ·0259 | ·0242 | ·0226 | ·0210 | ·0196 | ·0169 |
| 27 | ·0264 | ·0246 | ·0229 | ·0212 | ·0197 | ·0183 | ·0157 |
| 28 | ·0251 | ·0233 | ·0216 | ·0200 | ·0185 | ·0171 | ·0146 |
| 29 | ·0239 | ·0221 | ·0204 | ·0189 | ·0174 | ·0160 | ·0136 |
| 30 | ·0228 | ·0210 | ·0194 | ·0178 | ·0164 | ·0151 | ·0126 |
| 31 | ·0217 | ·0200 | ·0184 | ·0169 | ·0154 | ·0141 | ·0118 |
| 32 | ·0208 | ·0190 | ·0174 | ·0160 | ·0146 | ·0133 | ·0110 |
| 33 | ·0199 | ·0182 | ·0166 | ·0151 | ·0137 | ·0125 | ·0103 |
| 34 | ·0190 | ·0173 | ·0158 | ·0143 | ·0130 | ·0118 | ·0096 |
| 35 | ·0182 | ·0165 | ·0150 | ·0136 | ·0123 | ·0111 | ·0090 |
| 36 | ·0175 | ·0158 | ·0143 | ·0129 | ·0116 | ·0104 | ·0084 |
| 37 | ·0167 | ·0151 | ·0136 | ·0122 | ·0110 | ·0098 | ·0079 |
| 38 | ·0161 | ·0145 | ·0130 | ·0116 | ·0104 | ·0093 | ·0074 |
| 39 | ·0154 | ·0138 | ·0124 | ·0111 | ·0099 | ·0088 | ·0069 |
| 40 | ·0148 | ·0133 | ·0118 | ·0105 | ·0093 | ·0083 | ·0065 |
| 41 | ·0143 | ·0127 | ·0113 | ·0100 | ·0089 | ·0078 | ·0061 |
| 42 | ·0137 | ·0122 | ·0108 | ·0095 | ·0084 | ·0074 | ·0057 |
| 43 | ·0132 | ·0117 | ·0103 | ·0091 | ·0080 | ·0070 | ·0053 |
| 44 | ·0127 | ·0112 | ·0099 | ·0087 | ·0076 | ·0066 | ·0050 |
| 45 | ·0123 | ·0108 | ·0095 | ·0083 | ·0072 | ·0063 | ·0047 |
| 46 | ·0118 | ·0104 | ·0091 | ·0079 | ·0068 | ·0059 | ·0044 |
| 47 | ·0114 | ·0100 | ·0087 | ·0075 | ·0065 | ·0056 | ·0041 |
| 48 | ·0110 | ·0096 | ·0083 | ·0072 | ·0062 | ·0053 | ·0039 |
| 49 | ·0106 | ·0092 | ·0080 | ·0069 | ·0059 | ·0050 | ·1037 |
| 50 | ·0103 | ·0089 | ·0076 | ·0066 | ·0056 | ·0048 | ·0034 |

TABLE III.—*continued.*

SINKING FUND.—ANNUAL INVESTMENT TO PRODUCE £1 IN A TERM OF YEARS.

*For Explanation, see p.* 60.

| Years. | 2½ per cent. | 3 per cent. | 3½ per cent. | 4 per cent. | 4½ per cent. | 5 per cent. | 6 per cent. |
|---|---|---|---|---|---|---|---|
| 51 | 0·0100 | 0·0085 | 0·0073 | 0·0063 | 0·0053 | 0·0045 | 0·0032 |
| 52 | ·0096 | ·0082 | ·0070 | ·0060 | ·0051 | ·0043 | ·0030 |
| 53 | ·0093 | ·0079 | ·0067 | ·0057 | ·0048 | ·0041 | ·0029 |
| 54 | ·0089 | ·0076 | ·0065 | ·0055 | ·0046 | ·0039 | ·0027 |
| 55 | ·0087 | ·0073 | ·0062 | ·0052 | ·0044 | ·0037 | ·0025 |
| 56 | ·0084 | ·0071 | ·0060 | ·0050 | ·0042 | ·0035 | ·0024 |
| 57 | ·0081 | ·0068 | ·0057 | ·0048 | ·0040 | ·0033 | ·0022 |
| 58 | ·0078 | ·0066 | ·0055 | ·0046 | ·0038 | ·0031 | ·0021 |
| 59 | ·0076 | ·0064 | ·0053 | ·0044 | ·0036 | ·0030 | ·0020 |
| 60 | ·0074 | ·0061 | ·0051 | ·0042 | ·0035 | ·0028 | ·0019 |
| 61 | ·0071 | ·0059 | ·0049 | ·0040 | ·0033 | ·0027 | ·0018 |
| 62 | ·0069 | ·0057 | ·0047 | ·0039 | ·0031 | ·0026 | ·0017 |
| 63 | ·0067 | ·0055 | ·0045 | ·0037 | ·0030 | ·0024 | ·0016 |
| 64 | ·0065 | ·0053 | ·0044 | ·0035 | ·0029 | ·0023 | ·0015 |
| 65 | ·0063 | ·0051 | ·0042 | ·0034 | ·0027 | ·0022 | ·0014 |
| 66 | ·0061 | ·0050 | ·0040 | ·0033 | ·0026 | ·0021 | ·0013 |
| 67 | ·0059 | ·0048 | ·0039 | ·0031 | ·0025 | ·0020 | ·0012 |
| 68 | ·0057 | ·0046 | ·0037 | ·0030 | ·0024 | ·2019 | ·0012 |
| 69 | ·0056 | ·0045 | ·0036 | ·0029 | ·0023 | ·0018 | ·0011 |
| 70 | ·0054 | ·0043 | ·0035 | ·0027 | ·0022 | ·0017 | ·0010 |
| 71 | ·0052 | ·0042 | ·0033 | ·0026 | ·0021 | ·0016 | ·0010 |
| 72 | ·0051 | ·0041 | ·0032 | ·0025 | ·0020 | ·0015 | ·0009 |
| 73 | ·0049 | ·0039 | ·0031 | ·0024 | ·0019 | ·0015 | ·0009 |
| 74 | ·0948 | ·0038 | ·0030 | ·0023 | ·0018 | ·0014 | ·0008 |
| 75 | ·0047 | ·0037 | ·0029 | ·0022 | ·0017 | ·0013 | ·0008 |
| 76 | ·0045 | ·0035 | ·0028 | ·0021 | ·0016 | ·0013 | ·0007 |
| 77 | ·0044 | ·0034 | ·0027 | ·0021 | ·0016 | ·0012 | ·0007 |
| 78 | ·0043 | ·0033 | ·0026 | ·0020 | ·0015 | ·0011 | ·0006 |
| 79 | ·0041 | ·0032 | ·0025 | ·0019 | ·0014 | ·0011 | ·0006 |
| 80 | ·0040 | ·0031 | ·0024 | ·0018 | ·0014 | ·0010 | ·0006 |
| 81 | ·0039 | ·0030 | ·0023 | ·0017 | ·0013 | ·0010 | ·0005 |
| 82 | ·0038 | ·0029 | ·0022 | ·0017 | ·0013 | ·0009 | ·0005 |
| 83 | ·0037 | ·0028 | ·0021 | ·0016 | ·0012 | ·0009 | ·0005 |
| 84 | ·0036 | ·0027 | ·0021 | ·0015 | ·0011 | ·0008 | ·0005 |
| 85 | ·0035 | ·0026 | ·0020 | ·0015 | ·0011 | ·0008 | ·0004 |
| 86 | ·0034 | ·0026 | ·0019 | ·0014 | ·0010 | ·0008 | ·0004 |
| 87 | ·0033 | ·0025 | ·0019 | ·0014 | ·0010 | ·0007 | ·0004 |
| 88 | ·0032 | ·0024 | ·0018 | ·0013 | ·0010 | ·0007 | ·0004 |
| 89 | ·0031 | ·0023 | ·0017 | ·0013 | ·0009 | ·0007 | ·0003 |
| 90 | ·0030 | ·0023 | ·0017 | ·0012 | ·0009 | ·0006 | ·0003 |
| 91 | ·0030 | ·0022 | ·0016 | ·0012 | ·0008 | ·0006 | ·0003 |
| 92 | ·0029 | ·0021 | ·0015 | ·0011 | ·0008 | ·0006 | ·0003 |
| 93 | ·0028 | ·0021 | ·0015 | ·0011 | ·0008 | ·0005 | ·0003 |
| 94 | ·0027 | ·0020 | ·0014 | ·0010 | ·0007 | ·0005 | ·0003 |
| 95 | ·0026 | ·0019 | ·0014 | ·0010 | ·0007 | ·0005 | ·0002 |
| 96 | ·0026 | ·0019 | ·0013 | ·0010 | ·0007 | ·0005 | ·0002 |
| 97 | ·0025 | ·0018 | ·0013 | ·0009 | ·0006 | ·0004 | ·0002 |
| 98 | ·0024 | ·0018 | ·0012 | ·0009 | ·0006 | ·0004 | ·0002 |
| 99 | ·0024 | ·0017 | ·0012 | ·0008 | ·0006 | ·0004 | ·0002 |
| 100 | ·0023 | ·0016 | ·0012 | ·0008 | ·0006 | ·0004 | ·0002 |

# TABLE IV.

## LEASEHOLD ASSURANCE.—ANNUAL PREMIUMS TO SECURE £100 PAYABLE AT THE END OF A FIXED TERM OF YEARS.

(ATLAS ASSURANCE COMPANY, 1893.)

*For Explanation, see p.* 61.

| Term of years. | Rate per cent. | Term of years. | Rate per cent. | Term of years. | Rate per cent. |
|---|---|---|---|---|---|
| | £ s. d. | | £ s. d. | | £ s. d. |
| 10 | 8 9 5 | 40 | 1 5 10 | 70 | 0 8 6 |
| 11 | 7 11 8 | 41 | 1 4 9 | 71 | 0 8 2 |
| 12 | 6 16 10 | 42 | 1 3 9 | 72 | 0 7 11 |
| 13 | 6 4 9 | 43 | 1 2 9 | 73 | 0 7 8 |
| 14 | 5 13 8 | 44 | 1 1 10 | 74 | 0 7 5 |
| 15 | 5 4 5 | 45 | 1 1 0 | 75 | 0 7 2 |
| 16 | 4 16 4 | 46 | 1 0 1 | 76 | 0 6 11 |
| 17 | 4 9 3 | 47 | 0 19 5 | 77 | 0 6 8 |
| 18 | 4 3 0 | 48 | 0 18 8 | 78 | 0 6 6 |
| 19 | 3 17 4 | 49 | 0 17 11 | 79 | 0 6 3 |
| 20 | 3 12 4 | 50 | 0 17 3 | 80 | 0 6 1 |
| 21 | 3 7 9 | 51 | 0 16 8 | 81 | 0 5 10 |
| 22 | 3 3 8 | 52 | 0 16 0 | 82 | 0 5 8 |
| 23 | 2 19 11 | 53 | 0 15 5 | 83 | 0 5 6 |
| 24 | 2 16 5 | 54 | 0 14 10 | 84 | 0 5 4 |
| 25 | 2 13 4 | 55 | 0 14 4 | 85 | 0 5 2 |
| 26 | 2 10 5 | 56 | 0 13 10 | 86 | 0 5 0 |
| 27 | 2 7 9 | 57 | 0 13 4 | 87 | 0 4 10 |
| 28 | 2 5 3 | 58 | 0 12 10 | 88 | 0 4 8 |
| 29 | 2 3 0 | 59 | 0 12 5 | 89 | 0 4 7 |
| 30 | 2 0 10 | 60 | 0 12 0 | 90 | 0 4 5 |
| 31 | 1 18 10 | 61 | 0 11 6 | 91 | 0 4 3 |
| 32 | 1 17 0 | 62 | 0 11 2 | 92 | 0 4 2 |
| 33 | 1 15 4 | 63 | 0 10 9 | 93 | 0 4 0 |
| 34 | 1 13 8 | 64 | 0 10 5 | 94 | 0 3 11 |
| 35 | 1 12 2 | 65 | 0 10 0 | 95 | 0 3 9 |
| 36 | 1 10 9 | 66 | 0 9 8 | 96 | 0 3 8 |
| 37 | 1 9 5 | 67 | 0 9 4 | 97 | 0 3 6 |
| 38 | 1 8 1 | 68 | 0 9 0 | 98 | 0 3 5 |
| 39 | 1 6 11 | 69 | 0 8 9 | 99 | 0 3 4 |

SURRENDER VALUE.—The Directors guarantee to return the whole of the remiums paid, except the first, with 2 per cent. compound interest, if at any time he assured wish to surrender the policy.

# PART II.

# VALUATION.

## CHAPTER VII.

### DIFFERENT KINDS OF VALUE DEFINED.

"VALUE" is a term which has different significations according to the circumstances in which it is used. Thus, there may be the value to a vendor of a property taken by Compulsory purchase; there is the value as between *See page* 79. Partners of a factory or business in full operation, or of the same factory as a "Going concern" to a purchaser who *See page* 79. will have the advantages of the established management and connection; there is the Rateable value; there is the *See page* 105. value of the factory as a whole if it has Stopped working; *See page* 92. the value of what has been destroyed by Fire may have to *See page* 99. be appraised; there is again the value of the Land, Buildings, and Plant if dismantled and sold separately; and finally *See page* 96 there is the value, generally the lowest of all, obtainable by a Forced sale. These various kinds of value are referred to in the succeeding chapters.

**Price, how determined.**

The value of anything is sometimes defined as that which it will fetch: and in the sale of a factory, the price at any particular time will, if there be freedom on both sides, depend not on the original cost or on any arbitrary standard of value—although of course the cost at which a similar factory could be built and equipped is an important consi-

**Compulsory purchase.** *See page* 79.

deration—but on the competition either of buyers or sellers, in other words on the supply and demand. The element of freedom is wanting in a compulsory purchase; there, the basis of price is the value to the seller, who is compensated for what he loses and not for what the buyer gains.

**Value depends on earning power, and on past profits.**

The real basis of value, however, which generally guides a purchaser, is the estimated earning power, or the net revenue, past, present, and prospective, so far as it can be ascertained. From this point of view there is often more scope for difference of opinion than would at first sight appear. The rate of profit in the past is a primary basis, but this is not conclusive. A purchaser may see his way to improved methods, to an extended trade, or to a better utilisation of the plant, and so to greater profits. On the other hand, past profits may have been largely due to special knowledge of the proprietors, and much may really have been owing to skilled management, which, if obtainable at all in the future, may involve the payment of considerable salaries taking precedence of profits.

**Expenses of management.**

**Gross income and cost of maintenance.** *See page* 4.

Again, the profits of the past may have been due to favourable circumstances which have been altered; or may have been earned under a limited or wasting tenure; or the past income as shown by books of account may have been unduly swelled or diminished by a wrong estimate of depreciation. The net profits may have been kept low by a too liberal writing off for wear and tear; and a new proprietor may see his way to a higher revenue by diminishing this annual charge. On the other hand, if the value of plant be taken too high, the gross profits will in the future have not only to bear the cost of a proper and higher rate of depreciation, but may have to pay off, in extensive repairs and renewals, an accumulation of past neglect.

**No fixed rules for rates of profit.**

There is no fixed rule for the percentage of profit which

will induce capitalists to embark in a manufacturing trade. The regularity of the trade, the chances of occasional high profits, the accompanying risks of loss, the locality in which the business is carried on, and the indirect advantages or drawbacks attending it, are all circumstances which may tempt or repel different persons. It may be said, generally, that the tendency of profits in England has been downwards, and just as the return on the more secure investments in Government funds or railway debentures is by the growth of accumulated capital ever becoming lower, so in a different range, the profits of manufacturers tend to diminish.

**Profits tend to diminish like interest of money.**

On the other hand, as during a period of depression certain factories become quite unprofitable or losing concerns and are closed, the recollection of such unprofitable work disinclines investors from re-embarking in similar undertakings when trade improves, so that the surviving concerns which have been maintained in working order reap a greater profit because the competition is less than formerly. Or even if a succession of good years induces competition, so much time is spent in equipping and starting new works that the older undertakings are able to reap all the profit of the renewed demand before the new works are ready.

**Previous bad years lessen present value.**

*See page* 74.

But while considerations of this sort have full weight with a prudent purchaser, the selling value of a factory depends greatly on the briskness of trade at the time of sale; and a seller may legitimately take the advantage of higher prices that are ruling, and of the consequent inclination of purchasers to invest in such property. When the profits have been high, attention is directed to the trade in question; capitalists are inclined to embark in it; there are more buyers, and competition is favourable to the seller. The reverse occurs during a time of depression, and then, if a sale must be effected, the buyer has his opportunity.

**Price determined by briskness of trade.**

**Readiness for use enhances value.**
*See page* 92.

If transferred at a time of high prices, the real value depends mainly on the readiness of the factory. If because of high prices, capitalists begin to build new works, it will often be found that by the time they are ready prices have fallen, probably because new factories have increased the productive power, or even because the mere prospect of new factories induces competitors to lower their demands. If, however, a factory or any other undertaking can be bought in full working order, it may be profitable to pay a high price for it, so as to reap the immediate advantage. In the lace trade, for instance, the whole cost of the machinery may be recovered in one or two prosperous years, and therefore at a time of great demands and inflated prices it is not the intrinsic value of the machines which determines their price, but their immediate readiness for use.

**High purchase-price repaid by profits.**

So in the coal trade, when prices are exceptionally good, the owner or purchaser of a colliery in full working order may reap such profits as will recoup him for a high capital outlay; but if the profits so gained tempt others to re-open a disused colliery which has been allowed to fall into disrepair, or which is flooded with water, probably by the time there is coal to sell, prices will be low.

**High prices are only transient.**

When the nominal or current prices for any product of manufacture are very high, it will generally be found that these high prices are being paid only in a small proportion of cases, because the demand has outrun the supply; and it is because most manufacturers are already occupied with contracts taken at old rates that famine prices can be secured by the fortunate few who are free to undertake new work. And directly the others get rid of old contracts and are ready to reap the high rates, their very readiness causes the high rates to vanish. On the other hand, it is in a time of deep depression that prudent pur-

**Factories cheaply bought in dull times.**

chasers will often find the best opportunity for buying or building a factory.

The circumstances which determine the Value of a factory are numerous and varied, but they may be broadly divided into two classes, general and particular. The former are of a wide kind and relate to the amount of Capital required and the manner in which it is to be provided; also to the Locality of the factory, the Tenure under which it is held, and to any Advantages which the district or site possesses for the trade in question. The second class of circumstances are those pertaining immediately to the Factory itself, its Buildings and Plant.

**Value of a factory how determined.**

**Locality.**

*See page* 124.

The modern tendency towards large factories in which labour-saving processes are extensively adopted, increases the amount of Capital required for profitable working.

**Capital outlay.**

A bold expenditure may give the command of trade to those who have incurred it, even if in dull times the large current outlay for expenses can only be met by securing orders at or below cost price. It is this necessity of maintaining a large output in order to pay current expenses without regard to profit, that in a time of depressed trade forces prices down to a level ruinous to ordinary traders.

**Bold expenditure may give control of trade.**

On the other hand, while advantages due to skill and forethought rather than to expenditure of money are unquestionable, costly appliances may prove a cause of loss rather than of gain in dull times. For instance, a factory may be constructed with an output capacity of one ton of product per week for each £100 invested, as compared with existing and smaller factories which have cost £120 per unit of output. Moreover, the labour in the new factory may be only £3 per ton of finished product as compared with £3 10*s*. in the older factories. But it is possible that

**Costly plant may be a cause of failure.**

**Large factories burdensome when only half employed.**

this low cost can only be maintained when the factory is in full work, and that when it is only employed at one-half or one-third of its capacity, the proportions may be altered. The expensive labour-saving machinery must remain as a burden which cannot well be got rid of, while workmen may be discharged in the smaller factory. Factories so established may eventually repay those who can afford to wait; but without a large trade the burden of capital, especially if some of it be borrowed, is a frequent cause of failure.

*See pages* 21, 77, 93.

Ultimately the profit is reaped by those who take advantage of the failure to buy the factory for much less than it has cost; and instances occur of a second or even a third change of ownership before the capital can be brought down to a sum on which the earnings will allow a profit.

**Working capital.**

Not only the capital sunk in the factory itself, and in the purchase of goodwill, but the Working Capital which the business will require, is a question of great importance as determining the value of the undertaking to a new-comer. There is a wide range in the proportion which liquid capital bears to sunk capital in different trades. In some the operations of manufacture are speedy, the profits are earned quickly, and the turnover of capital is correspondingly frequent. In such cases, if the cost of material form the chief part of the total outlay, a large business may sometimes be conducted with moderate capital, because the material need not be paid for till the finished product is sold. But Wages need ready money, and hence it is that when the cost of labour forms a considerable proportion of the whole, a large liquid capital is necessary, and profits must correspond. Thus, while a miller, or a maltster, or a sugar refiner may sell his products within a month of purchasing his wheat or barley or sugar, and at a price only slightly above the cost of the raw material, a maker of locomotives may have to pay for his iron, steel, and copper many months before he obtains repayment; and

**Quick turnover.**

**Wages outlay.**

**Liquid capital.**

moreover during that period will have had to pay in weekly wages three times the value of these raw materials.

**Borrowed money.** *See pages* 21, 93.

The proportion which Borrowed Money may safely bear to the capital of the proprietors is also a matter of great importance, and it obviously depends on ever-varying circumstances for which no rule is possible. The risk of failure from this cause may be minimised by using only those forms of borrowing which, though conceding a higher rate of interest or a preferential share of profit, do not involve any sudden demands for repayment, rather than by borrowing at a low rate, with the risk of repayment being demanded at a short notice.

**Risks may be avoided.** *See page* 123.

**Tenure limited by lease.**

The tenure of a factory or other industrial undertaking may be limited by lease of buildings or land, or by the terms of a charter or concession, or by the wasting nature of the property as in the case of mines already referred to. If the earnings before being applicable to the payment of interest or dividend have to bear the burden of a sinking fund for a recovery of the capital, it is obviously the net income alone which must form the basis for calculating the value. Manufactories dependent for their profits on patents or other monopolies of a temporary kind have a limited value accordingly. But if the vendors have already established a sinking fund according to the system of Leasehold Assurance, the annual premiums to maintain the Policy of Assurance may be a much less burden on the purchaser than if the latter had to inaugurate a sinking fund. The handing over such a policy by the vendor when transferring the business will go far to make it equal to a freehold or permanent undertaking.

**Sinking fund.** *See page* 60.

**Leasehold assurance.** *See page* 60.

**Locality.** *See page* 124.

The question of Locality is dealt with in a separate chapter, but it may be remarked here that in dealing with an existing business the situation of the factory may usually be regarded as no longer an open question, and any advantages or drawbacks which the factory may possess in this respect, though they may increase or diminish its value, cannot be altered. This is so in the great majority of cases; but when a business is valuable in other respects; when for instance, there is an established organisation, an experienced staff, as well as a reputation or connection among customers, it may prove remunerative to buy

**Factory may be removed.**

*See page* 29.

such a business, if only to remove it wholly or partially to a different locality. Such a change is of course encouraged if the existing factory, or the site, has a realisable value for other purposes; and the feasibility of a change in case of need is of importance where a factory is held on a lease soon to terminate.

## CHAPTER VIII.

### THE VALUE OF A FACTORY AS A GOING CONCERN.

IN the purchase of a factory as "a Going concern," or in its valuation on this basis, circumstances have to be considered which do not always present themselves in the annual stock-taking. The Capital as it stands in the books of account does not necessarily represent the Real Value, which, when measured by the past, present, or prospective Earning Capacity of the undertaking, may be greater or less than the nominal or assumed value. A purchaser is the more anxious to be assured on this point because there is the natural conjecture that if the undertaking were profitable the proprietor would not desire to sell it. An explanation why the factory is offered for sale is generally therefore the preliminary step in the transaction.

**Value measured by earning capacity.**

**Reasons for selling required**

In regard to Compulsory Purchase, where the purchaser rather than the vendor desires the transfer, it is the value to the vendor which determines the price. For as in the case of purchase by a railway company or municipality who wish to occupy the site, much of what the vendor loses may have no value to the buyer, as for instance the connection or goodwill, which may be jeopardised or lessened by removal. There is the marked difference between compulsory purchases of this kind by public bodies and purchases by traders, that the seller is free to commence working elsewhere and retains all the goodwill he can in removing to new premises.

**Compulsory purchase.**

**Seller retains goodwill.**

*See page* 84.

It is seldom, except in a retail trade, that much of the goodwill is lost by a mere removal to another and adjacent

**Loss by removal.**

**Compensation for damage.**

situation ; but a factory owner is entitled to Compensation for the expense and trouble of Removal, for the Damage caused to plant and stock, for the cost of Adapting his plant to new premises, for the Storage of his machinery and stock till he has obtained a new site, and for the loss of Profit till he can recommence working. Not only the past and present rate of profit must be taken into account, but the likelihood of a prospective increase ; and the seller is entitled to the capitalised value of what he is losing, subject to a deduction for what he may be likely to earn under altered circumstances. When all these points have been taken into account and a total sum arrived at, the vendor is entitled to a further sum for the compulsory nature of the sale ; and by practice and precedent 10 per cent. on the total is the amount which judges or arbitrators allow, and which sellers always claim.

**Prospective profits.**

**Compensation for compulsion.**

**Sale of public works to municipal bodies.**

A very different basis of value obtains in the sale of public works such as town tramways, markets, and electric lighting undertakings, where the municipal authorities in granting the original charter or concession, have reserved the right to acquire the undertaking on favourable terms. Although in foreign countries concessions for limited periods of years have long been customary — railways, gas-works, and water-works being established on such conditions — it was in Great Britian a somewhat new departure when the system of optional purchase was inaugurated for town tramways. In the 44th section of the London Street Tramways Act 1870, it was prescribed that the Local Authorities might, on the expiration of twenty-one years from the construction of the tramway, "require such promoters to sell to them their undertaking, or so much of the same as is within such district, upon terms of paying them their value (exclusive of any allowance for past or future profits of the undertaking, or any compensation for compulsory sale or other consideration what-

**Concessions for terms of years.**

**London Tramways.**

**Option of purchase.**

soever) of the tramway, and all lands, buildings, works, materials, and plant of the promoters suitable to and used by them for the purpose of their undertaking within such district, such value to be, in case of difference, determined by an engineer or other fit person nominated as referee on the application of either party." In the year 1891 the London County Council resolved to exercise its right to purchase about 4¼ miles, or nearly a third of the company's system, which had been twenty-one years in existence. As the first occasion on which such a principle of valuation was to be applied, considerable interest was taken by all those who had embarked capital in similar undertakings.

**First purchase under these conditions.**

**By London County Council.**

Sir Frederick Bramwell, the umpire appointed under the Act, issued his award in March 1893, as follows:—"I determine and award that the sum of £64,540 is the value of the purchased tramways and the works thereof (other than such works as are comprised in the annexed agreement), exclusive of any allowance for past or future profits of the undertaking or any compensation for compulsory purchase, or other consideration whatever, except the consideration of the value to the Tramways Company or to the County Council, measured by what it would cost either the Tramways Company or the County Council to establish the purchased tramways if such tramways do not now exist, but taking into account a proper deduction in respect of depreciation. And, accordingly, I determine and award that the value of the purchased tramways, and of all lands, buildings, works, materials, and plant of the tramways company, suitable to and used by them for the purpose of the undertaking of the purchased tramways, as such purchased tramways, lands, buildings, works, materials, and plant are defined by the annexed agreement, is the sum of £64,540, together with the further sum or sums payable under the annexed agreement, and that such sum or sums together form the 'then value' of the premises

**Terms of award.**

**Basis of valuation.**

Costs of the award.

within the meaning of the 44th Section of 'The London Street Tramways Act, 1870.' And I award and direct that the County Council do pay to the Tramways Company the costs incurred by the Tramways Company of, and incidental to, the reference, and this award, including the proper expenses of the Tramways Company of, and incidental to, negotiating, preparing, and executing, the annexed agreement."

The agreement referred to in the above award provides *inter alia* for the Council acquiring certain depôts for sums in addition to that awarded, and also provides for the Council purchasing cars, harness, horses, &c., at a price to be determined "by some person practically acquainted with the value thereof."

Purchase of electric-lighting works by local authority.

Somewhat the same principle of compulsory expropriation was embodied in many of the Acts authorising Electric Lighting undertakings, the same reason prevailing, that it is to the general advantage that the roadways of a city shall be wholly under the control of the local authority, and that private companies shall not possess proprietary rights of any description in the public highway. But while this principle has been accepted as equitable, the length of term is a question for arrangement, and in the case of electric lighting a longer period has been allowed (forty years is a usual term) than was at first proposed.

Estimate of value qualified. *See page* 16.

Leaving aside, however, the special conditions attending a compulsory sale, whether favourable to the vendor or to the purchaser as above described, there have to be considered in valuing the undertaking as a whole for a free sale as a going concern the general circumstances already alluded to, which may qualify very considerably the total of the detailed estimate. Thus the value of the Land may have altered; the advantages of any Goodwill, Monopoly, or Privileges pertaining to the undertaking have to be considered, or Deductions may have to be made because of adverse changes in these respects.

**Value of site.** *See pages* 29, 106.

In regard to the Land it may be that the Site has grown in value for the particular trade, and that owing to some of the circumstances which determine the choice of locality the factory or undertaking may possess advantages over others engaged in a similar business. Certain trades have special localities, and inferior buildings if well situated may be more saleable and valuable than those well-built and equipped but wrongly placed. Past profits may in fact have been mainly due to these advantages of locality rather than to any in the factory itself.

**Local advantages.**

**Site valuable for other purposes.** *See page* 30.

If, however, the Site has grown in value not because of its suitability for the trade in question, but because of its situation in a town or city and its fitness for other kinds of buildings or for other purposes, then this increment may be an actual disadvantage to the factory, if owing to a fresh valuation on this basis it is burdened with a higher rent or interest on capital in consequence. But a site covered with factory buildings can seldom be utilised for other and more profitable purposes without dismantling; and loss in this direction may go far to balance the natural advantages of the site. A purchaser who intends to continue the business will be mainly guided by the earning power of the factory, and will not pay much regard to a prospective and problematical increase in the value of the land.

**Dismantling.** *See pages* 26, 96.

**Excessive price paid for site.** *See page* 30.

As an opposite case, a high price may have originally been paid for the land because of anticipated advantages which have not been realised; and an investigation may prove that for the particular purpose of the factory the book value of the land is excessive and must be diminished. It may be that an undertaking efficient in all other respects has been so burdened by the excessive capital account from this cause, or from a high ground-rent, that it has not proved profitable, and a reduction

**Heavy burden of ground rent.**

in capital value or in rent may be the condition of future prosperity.

**Factory sold as a Going concern.**

In the sale of a factory as a Going concern, if not only are there orders on the books, but also a list of customers who regularly buy at prices which afford profit to the manufacturer, in other words, if there be a "Goodwill," it is obvious that a certain live value is given to the undertaking, which it would not possess as a mere aggregation of buildings and plant. The special value from this cause must obviously vary. It may be that better prices are obtainable than in other and less known undertakings, or that in dull times the factory is likely to be fairly well employed when others are idle. And as, in calculating the net revenue obtainable from a business, it is the Average Profits which have to be considered, the probability of constant employment is of great importance. Advantages of this sort are not always directly represented in the books of account nor in the capital accounts of the partners, but they have a value to new purchasers as assuring a regularity of income. As, however, the permanence of such favourable conditions depends upon many future and unknown contingencies, their capitalised value must be calculated moderately.

**Goodwill.** *See page* 28.

**Goodwill valued by average profits.**

**Value of goodwill not shown in accounts.**

**Capitalised value.**

The Value of Goodwill depends to a considerable extent on the amount of capital required to carry on the factory; for, however well a business may be established, yet if in order to obtain the promised advantages a large amount of capital is required, the addition which the goodwill may be expected to make to the average revenue will be depreciated, even if interest on capital be deducted before reckoning the annual revenue. The plan is often adopted in the sale of a manufacturing business, of stating no separate price for goodwill, but of valuing the plant liberally on the assumption that profitable employment in the future is assured, while sometimes a premium is paid in addition for entering on the business.

**Value diminished if large working capital required.** *See pages* 76, 77.

**Premium paid on valuation.**

Goodwill, whether paid for directly or not, generally represents much past expenditure in the making of the business, and this, though it may have been prudently written off by the proprietors, as being represented by no material assets, may yet be legitimately charged to new-comers, who are to reap the advantages of it. But where such goodwill has been maintained by advertising or other active means, the value of the goodwill must not be reckoned without taking due account also of the expenditure for maintaining it. Where goodwill is separately appraised it seldom exceeds from one to three years' purchase of the net profit, after deducting 5 per cent. interest on the capital employed in the business.

**Goodwill valuable though written off.**

*See page* 27.

**Advertising.**

In regard to Monopolies arising from Patents, where a manufacturer is merely a licensee, his advantage depends upon the amount of competition by others who also have licences; and sometimes such competition is as severe as if no patent existed. But when the manufacturer has a monopoly of a patent, his profits may be large, and indeed are limited only by the demand of the purchasers. Even when the patent monopoly is at an end, the manufacturer whose name is associated with the goods, and who by years of use has his plant and processes well adapted, can generally work more cheaply than his competitors and retain in this way a partial monopoly for many years. But in the case of a widely known and important invention, like that of Bessemer steel or Telephones, the advantage ends with the term of the patent right, as outsiders are generally ready to use the invention immediately.

**Value of patent rights.**

*See page* 54.

**Monopoly may outlive patent.**

A Trade-mark may give a more permanent monopoly to the maker than a patent right limited to a term of years, because while, after the term expires, the right of manufacture becomes common, the monopoly of the trade-mark will remain. It is therefore generally advantageous to establish a trade-mark or brand while the patent is in

**Trade-marks.**

**Value, how limited.**

force. But obviously its value will continue only so long as the seller can induce the belief that his mark or guarantee is a more trustworthy certificate of quality than any appearance of similarity which may be given by others.

**Value of trade-mark abroad.**

Where the trade-mark is recognised in foreign countries, it often is valuable to the proprietors long after its value has lapsed in the country of manufacture.

**Secret processes.**

Sometimes a Monopoly depends neither on a patent nor a trade-mark, but on Secret processes of manufacture, or on the skill and experience of a limited number of workmen. The permanency of such a monopoly will then of course depend on the retention of such workmen, or the transmitting of their knowledge to others.

**Patentees who manufacture.**

The profits arising from the manufacture, and the advantages which may be expected to remain to those who have acquired experience in it, even after a patent has expired, sometimes induce patentees who are not manufacturers to establish a factory for carrying out their invention. This, however, frequently results in loss, for the functions of inventor and maker are quite distinct;

**Causes of non-success.**

the operations of making, buying, and selling require a special commercial experience; and moreover, the manufacture is generally carried on best by those who have other and kindred operations or branches of trade which utilise the same plant and organisation.

**Depreciated plant may have revived value to new-comer.**

The value of plant, as shown in the capital account of a factory which has been successfully managed, should be less than the real value to a new-comer who is to continue the business. Depreciation as treated in the accounts should not only balance the mere wear and tear, but provide for contingencies; and although partners, as between themselves, may have prudently written off on this basis, yet if, when the property is transferred, these contingencies have not occurred, the future risks no longer concern the sellers, who may justly retain what has in effect been an insurance or reserve fund. For instance, the value of patterns and other accessories may have been written down to little or nothing, because of a possible cessation in their usefulness, but if these accessories are still in use, the value to a new comer revives, and a new departure may be taken in the way of depreciation.

**Past depreciation enquired into.**

In view of certain scandals in the over-valuation of private undertakings sold to joint-stock companies a Bill was introduced in the Parliamentary Session of 1888 for amending the laws under which limited liability companies are formed, and amongst other reforms it was proposed that in any sale of a manufacturing undertaking past depreciation should be inquired into and notified. No enactment, however, was made.

## CHAPTER IX.

### THE RENTAL VALUE OF FACTORIES.

**Rental value.**

**Interest on cost varies with risk.**

*See page* 72.

IN the valuation of a factory as a going concern, it is sometimes desirable to arrive at its Rental Value. Different classes of buildings are supposed to yield certain rates of interest according to the trouble and risk attending them, and whatever may have been their original cost, purchasers will only value them on this basis.

**Occupying owners**

**allow for rent as interest on capital.**

Dwelling-houses and shops are usually let to tenants, and the amount paid in rent is, to the occupier, a distinct charge, which can be kept separate from all other outgoings. But in the case of Factories, the buildings are more often the property of the occupier, who in his annual accounts may either set down a sum for rent, or, including together all his outlay for land, buildings, and plant, may charge "interest on capital" on the whole; all of the net earnings which remain, after a sum has been set apart for depreciation, being treated as profit. Where one partner is the owner of a factory, a sum is paid or set apart as rent; where the partners are equally the owners, "interest on capital" is the usual method.

**Gross rent must allow for depreciation.**

In the case of a factory where the occupancy is assured for a term of years, and the rent is a first charge on profits, the rate of interest, to be an appropriate rate, should, so far as it applies to the buildings, be equal (including the depreciation rate) to the rental which a landlord who owned but did not occupy a factory would let it for. For assuming that in either case the occupier whether tenant or proprietor, did the repairs and paid for insurance against fire, then if $1\frac{1}{2}$ per cent. per annum were reserved for depreciation, this with 5 per cent. interest would be equal to a rent of $6\frac{1}{2}$ per cent. on the value.

*See page* 105.

**Factories let to working tenants.**

*See page* 111.

In certain trades where small factories or workshops are let out to working tenants, a much higher rate of interest than $6\frac{1}{2}$ per cent. on the cost is charged as rent; but this is generally because of special risks, such as of having the premises unlet in dull times, or of the occasional non-payment of rent, or of expenses in collecting it. There may also be risk of changes in trade which might render the factory less suitable, and therefore less secure as an investment, than ordinary house property. These circumstances do not weigh with equal force in the case of an occupying owner, but when they are incidental to the property, allowance would be made for them in determining the net rental value, just as in assessing for rating purposes.

**Rateable value.**

*See page* 106.

**Power included in rent.**

In some manufacturing towns, factories or blocks of workshops are let out on rent; sometimes power sufficient for one or more looms or other defined machinery is included in this rent; sometimes a constant power is specified, or that which can be transmitted by a shaft or belt or pulley of certain size, running at a certain speed. Sometimes, more often abroad than in England, power alone is sold at an annual rate, but in these cases the rental value of the building is increased because of the convenient contiguity of such power.

**Value of leases, how determined.**

In valuing a factory, the value of the building may, if taken separately from the plant, be reckoned on the rental basis as above. If the property is freehold or on a long lease, an addition may have to be made for prospective increase in value. If the property is held on lease only, then its freehold value must be diminished by the sum sufficient, if invested as a sinking fund, to repay at the end of the term the purchase money. Or the freehold value

**Sinking fund.**

*See page* 60.

may be diminished by the sum sufficient to buy a deferred annuity of the annual or net rental value, commencing at the end of the lease and continuing on in perpetuity. The cost of any obligations specified in the lease must also be provided for. But even with these allowances leaseholds do not fetch so high a price as freeholds. The convenience afforded by the system of leasehold assurance has been already referred to, and the annual premiums are given in Table IV.

*See page* 60.

**Local advantages.**

*See page* 124.

The Locality of the factory in regard to material, transport, and other circumstances, the general arrangement of workshops or other buildings, and the facilities afforded for the bringing in of material, for lifting and moving during the operations of manufacture, for the proper sequence of these operations, and for the delivery of the finished product, are all of importance in determining a rental value. In regard also to the plant, economy in working depends to a considerable extent on the order and arrangement of the machines and the mode of applying power to them. Besides the workmen immediately employed in the operations of manufacture, there is always accessory labour required, and accessory and unremunerative consumption of power. The loss of heat from the boilers and steam-pipes, the waste of power from ill-arranged engines, and the consumption of force by transmission-shafting, wheels, and pulleys, must always take place to a certain extent; the loss is sometimes excessive and unnecessary; and while in the laying out of a factory it is of course the object to minimise such loss, so in valuing an existing factory it is necessary to take it into account.

**Value depends on arrangement of plant.**

**Cost of labour increased by defective arrangements.**

**Delay and risk in building new factories.**

But in considering the rental value of an existing factory, however much it may be evident that a new factory would allow of improved arrangements, the fact that buildings and plant are already established is in itself of considerable value. The trouble, delay, and expense which always attend the designing of new works have been incurred, the risk of error has been run, and the buildings and plant have at any rate been proved by work actually done. The trouble and expense of fixing machinery add considerably to its cost, and generally more than the visible result discloses.

## CHAPTER X.

### THE VALUE OF A FACTORY THAT HAS STOPPED WORKING.

IN the valuation of a factory as a whole, but yet not as a going concern, the preliminary question arises, as alluded to in a preceding chapter: why, if the undertaking had been profitable or capable of producing profit, has it been stopped? There may be answers to this, such as the death of the proprietor, a temporary falling off in trade, or want of skill or attention in the management. Some industries are liable to periodical stoppages from economic causes, such as a falling demand for the products, or by a lowering of the market price below the cost of production, two circumstances not necessarily associated. As an example of the first are manufactures dependent on fashion, such as lace goods, which return a high rate of profit when trade is brisk.

*See page* 79.

**Periodical stoppages.**

**Trades dependent on fashion.**

Just as a falling off in the demand may cause factories to be closed, so the dormant value revives when the conditions of trade improve. The value then depends not only on the suitability of the factory, but on its readiness. Mining and metallurgical operations are often stopped because the selling price has fallen below the cost of production; and yet the plant may have been kept ready for future working. In some competing district the local advantages may overcome all competition, or the discovery of uses for by-products may so increase the total net return as to allow the chief or stable product to be sold at a lower

**Mining and metallurgical operations.**

**By-products.**

rate than formerly; or the staple article of manufacture itself may be produced elsewhere as a by-product at a low price. The mining for lead and silver, or for copper and sulphur, and the carrying on of industries connected with these minerals, are examples. Where the purchase of a mine or factory or other industrial undertaking that has stopped working is in question, investigation may disclose causes of this sort which are not immediately apparent.

**Silver and lead.**

**Copper and sulphur.**

A manufacturing business may often prove unsuccessful because of an excessive burden of capital. Where a factory and the capital necessary to work it are the unencumbered property of the occupiers, it may be expedient to continue working for a time for little or no profit, or at any rate till the profits become less than would be obtained as interest on the price of the factory if sold; but where the occupiers are working with borrowed money, or have to pay a preferential rent or interest, they may be unable to continue, and it will probably then be necessary for some of the capital to be cancelled to allow a profit on the remainder.

**Excessive capital a cause of non-success.**

*See page* 75.

**Borrowed capital.**

*See pages* 21, 77.

Assuming that a re-starting of the factory under new conditions appears justifiable, a stoppage may not have been altogether a disadvantage, for there is now an opportunity of resuming work clear of past mistakes and engagements. There may indeed be a loss of "goodwill," but this depends greatly on the nature of the trade and on how far that rests on old connections. The value of the foundations, attachments, and other accessories to plant and machinery already installed, of course remains good, and there is the advantage that repairs and re-arrangements can be made, which in a going concern would be difficult or impossible. But when machines have been stopped, an allowance may be necessary in the valuation to provide for risks or uncertainties attending a recommencement, while in a still going concern the machinery might be seen in operation. Most kinds of machinery are liable to deteriora-

**Opportunity for rectifying past mistakes.**

**Goodwill.**

*See pages* 28, 84.

**Allowance for risks in recommencing.**

tion by remaining idle; some kinds suffer more during such a period than by the operations of working.

**Factories retain substantial value in suitable locality.**

If a factory has been engaged in a staple trade and in a suitable locality, it will almost certainly retain a substantial value, though a favourable opportunity may have to be awaited to obtain a purchaser. The sale of a factory sometimes discloses that it has a value to some persons for reasons not affecting ordinary purchasers who look only to direct profit. Thus, a purchaser may have land or produce in the neighbourhood which is enhanced in value by the working of the factory or which would suffer loss by its stoppage; or he may have some manufacturing business complementary to that in question which will work well in connection with it. A public sale sometimes for reasons such as these elicits an unexpected competition.

**Special value to particular persons.**

**Factory may afford indirect profits.**

The stoppage of a factory may have caused such loss in its neighbourhood, that the owners of property, or tradesmen who have spare capital to invest, may be willing to share in the risk of re-establishing the business, even with the foreknowledge or probability of only a small return in interest, because they will benefit by the local expenditure in wages and the consequent effect on rents of houses, and other direct or indirect advantages.

*See page* 130.

**Value of machines, how arrived at.**

If the machines are appropriate for their purpose, then their value will be arrived at by adding to their original cost the expenses of installation, and deducting an amount for depreciation proportioned to their age and wear, and a further amount for any actual repairs they may require. It sometimes happens that a machine or apparatus has been so strengthened, improved, or added to, that it is really worth more than when new.

**Old plant valuable if undisturbed.**

There is often, in or about a factory, plant which is so old or worn that it would not bear removal, but which is likely to last a considerable time if left undisturbed.

Although the necessity for renewals when this time shall have expired may be obvious, it is often an advantage that the immediate capital outlay for the purchase of the factory is thus reduced and the purchase of new machines spread over a term of years.

Sometimes the machines may be too worn to do the best work in the factory, and yet be useful for second-class operations. But a distinction must be drawn between what is merely partially worn and what is obsolete. In trades where new labour-saving processes have been introduced, the free gift of certain machines, even though they be in good condition, would not prevent loss in using them if the labour attending their use much exceeded that in competing factories, or if they produced goods of an inferior quality. Such machines should be got rid of at whatever loss, and sold to those who could use them in kindred but less important operations.

**Obsolete machines valueless for use.**

*See page* 19.

Assuming that the factory in resuming work is to be employed in the same business as before, the value of the plant may be arrived at by the same process as in a going concern, but with this difference, that while in the latter a premium for goodwill may have to be paid, there may be, in the case of a factory that has stopped working, the need for some deduction to compensate for the time which may elapse before it is all employed.

**Goodwill.**

*See page* 93.

**Deduction for loss of time.**

If a change is to be made in the kind of goods manufactured, the value of the plant to a purchaser will be diminished by the cost of any alterations needed to render it suitable. Of course a seller may elect to refuse a price so diminished, and may prefer to wait for a purchaser who can use the factory for its proper purpose. But on the other hand, if any of the machines have become obsolete for their original employment, it will generally be to the seller's advantage that there be a change in the kind of goods to be manufactured.

**Allowance for alterations.**

**Value of plant enhanced by past reputation.**

A new-comer will be largely guided, in estimating the value of the plant, by the reputation of the factory for good work during its previous occupancy. So also, if the occupiers have had a character for skill and judgment, plant chosen and arranged by them will be deemed to have a value accordingly. On the other hand, if the stoppage of the factory is supposed to have been due to inefficient management, the plant may be liable to disparagement.

**or diminished by contrary cause.**

**Dismantlement.**

If a factory is Dismantled the plant almost necessarily loses by removal, the extent of the loss depending on the nature of the plant and its mode of attachment to the premises. In the first place, the capital sunk in foundations and attachments to the buildings is generally all lost; and from the value which the plant would then have for re-erection elsewhere must be deducted the cost of taking down, and the expenses and risks of removal. In the case of a self-contained machine depending very little on special attachment, the removal may be easy and the loss slight; in the case of machines or apparatus composed partly of brickwork, such as boilers and furnaces, the loss is very great.

**Foundations and accessories.**

**Loss by removal.**

**Special machines.**

A further depreciation is likely to occur if the machines have been made of special form or size to suit local peculiarities of land or buildings. Such special form may involve not only cutting to waste to allow of re-use, as in the case of shafting, piping, and belting, but actuai alterations to suit a new situation. Original simplicity of design minimises the loss from such causes.

**Loss by alteration.**

**Machines in common use sell best.**

*See page* 18.

As a rule, that plant sells best which is in common use for many trades. Thus a portable engine or an ordinary drilling-machine or screw-cutting lathe will find generally more bidders than an air-compressor or a deep-well pump. There are, however, exceptions to this rule, there sometimes being a keen competition for special machines not easily procurable new, such occasions arising oftenest when the trade in question is brisk. Manufacturers who see their way to immediate profit by adding to their plant, may be eager to buy what is at once available, when a similar but new machine could not instantly be got ready. Thus it is often expedient to await a favourable opportunity for the disposal of old plant rather than to force an immediate sale.

**Readiness of second-hand plant is sometimes valuable.**
*See page* 74.

The minimum value of any second-hand plant is that of the old material it contains, less the cost of removal and breaking up. The maximum value is that of a similar article new, immediately obtainable. In the range between these two extremes, the actual price depends on collateral circumstances. Thus there is the locality of the sale. If it is in a town or district where there are numerous persons engaged in the same or kindred trades, there are likely to be more bidders than under contrary conditions, for a large or important sale is necessary to tempt purchasers to a distance. It may even be expedient to remove the plant to a more favourable locality, but this is generally expensive and is rarely adopted.

**Minimum and maximum value.**
*See page* 35.

**Locality of sale.**

**Removal of plant for sale.**

The best prices are generally offered by those who intend themselves to use what they buy. Failing such purchasers, the sale depends on Dealers, who buy to sell again, and a new set of circumstances determines price, for a dealer requires an intermediate profit and has also to consider not merely the cost of removal, but that of storage, the loss of interest while waiting for a customer, the risk of deterioration by time, or of improvements being introduced which will render the plant he has purchased obsolete, and the ultimate contingency of having to realise only the scrap or old-material value.

**Value to users and dealers.**

In a sale to dealers, the name and reputation of the original maker of the goods have a special value. For, while the first purchaser sees the machine in place with

**Name of original maker affects value.**

evidence of its having been usefully at work, a chance purchaser from the store of the dealer will have to be guided to a greater extent by the name or brand or trade-mark of the maker. This circumstance should not be lost sight of by purchasers of new plant, who may with advantage choose what will retain the best value in case of re-sale. Contractors for public works who buy plant for use in one contract only, and who from its commencement look forward to a re-sale, in which indeed much of their profit or loss is involved, have generally this circumstance in view when they purchase locomotives, steam-cranes, or other important plant.

**Re-sale of contractor's plant.**

**Dealers can sometimes pay more than users.**

On the other hand, dealers can sometimes afford to pay more than users. They may command a wider circle of purchasers than are present at the sale; they may know of customers seeking what is now offered; or they may see their way by a moderate expenditure to give a more than corresponding improvement to their purchase.

**Sale without reserve.**

A sale without reserve may involve heavy loss to the sellers, and it is generally endeavoured to avoid it by placing a reserve price on what is to be sold. The post-ponement of a sale is, however, rendered difficult when the articles are heavy or cumbrous, and when a peremptory removal is necessary. In cases of this sort, as also in that of improper collusion among bidders, much depends upon the ability and experience of the auctioneer.

# CHAPTER XI.

## THE VALUATION OF LOSSES BY FIRE.

THE principle of Fire insurance, according to the practice of all English offices, is that of Indemnity, and not, as in the case of either marine or life insurance, the payment of a fixed sum agreed upon beforehand. For example, if a factory which has been insured for £1000 be wholly or partially destroyed by fire, the amount of the loss will have to be appraised, and only the actual amount of loss, with a maximum of £1000, will be paid. The assured have to produce as particular an account of their loss as the nature of the case permits, according to the terms of the policy; and in the case of a factory containing plant of fluctuating value, the making up of an equitable claim for loss by fire needs considerable care.

**Indemnity the basis of insurance.**

**Loss must be appraised.**

It is often difficult after a fire to make up an exact estimate of loss. If the books and papers are preserved, invoices and other vouchers will probably be available to show the cost of the plant, material, and stock as they entered the factory. If these vouchers have been lost in the fire, then outside evidence from those who supplied the plant and goods will have to be collected as the basis of a claim.

**Difficult to estimate loss.**

**Vouchers to prove loss.**

The value of the property immediately anterior to the fire is that on which the estimate of loss must be based, and as it is the current or market value of the articles consumed, and not the original price of them, any rise or fall of value takes effect, and the assured is paid accordingly.

**Value defined and limited.**

**Depreciation.** *See page* 15. **Reinstatement.**

Thus the question of Depreciation necessarily arises, for an insurance office does not undertake to reinstate or to provide new buildings and plant in the place of old ones. An analogous case arises in marine insurance, where, if a ship be damaged, the underwriters in paying the cost of repairs deduct, unless the ship be new, one-third, on the ground that the substitution of new for old material is a benefit to the shipowner.

**Accessories included in loss.**

Subject to the total amount recovered not exceeding that on the policy, the assured is entitled to the value of plant equipped as at the time of the fire, and therefore all cost of foundations and attachments, as well as the cost of installation, have to be included. The assured is also entitled to the cost of removing the *débris*. On these bases, and allowing for possible deduction for depreciation, the sum paid should be sufficient for the reinstatement of the factory. In regard to deductions which may be claimed by the insurance office on account of the worn condition of the buildings or plant, the assured may be called upon to furnish information as to the length of time the factory and plant, or any part of them, have been in operation; and in this respect English offices generally deal liberally with the assured.

**Deductions for wear and tear.**

*See page* 15.

Those who have an old factory, and who have written off little or nothing for depreciation, may find that the sum recoverable leaves them deficient of the capital value recorded in their books of account. If any of the plant has become obsolete, such a fact will also be taken into account as reducing its original value; and patent rights which may have increased the original cost, but which have since lapsed, will not be allowed for.

On the other hand, if it can be shown that the plant which has been destroyed was, by reason of its kind or arrangement, of greater value than when first purchased, the assured will be entitled to a corresponding compensation. Where plant has been regularly depreciated, it does not follow that only the value as so lessened can be claimed. Depreciation is, after all, but an estimate of what may be necessary to meet contingencies, some of them of a speculative kind, and as the losses provided against may have been escaped, a review of all the circumstances, so far as they can be ascertained, may show a higher value than is stated in accounts drawn up for a different purpose. Surveyors or engineers accustomed to the class of property destroyed are generally employed to appraise the loss, and in case of dispute arbitration is resorted to, the right to such a mode of settlement being generally reserved by the insurance office in the policy.

**Past depreciation revised.**

*See page* 24.

**Value may be more than shown in books of account.**

Sometimes the valuation is assisted by the fulness of the description of the property which has been furnished to the insurance office at the time the policy was issued, but in the case of a factory with a constantly fluctuating amount of plant, it is seldom that everything can be set down in advance, nor can the absence of such a detailed description bar the claim of the assured.

**Valuation assisted by description supplied by assured.**

There are, however, certain kinds of property which must be classed separately, and a maximum value set upon them at the time of insurance. Such, for instance, are drawings if they exceed a trifling amount, patterns, models, and moulds, which in the engineering and other trades may have a special value. Not only must a maximum total value be stated, but the insurance office will limit the sum payable on any one such article.

**Drawings and models classed separately.**

In the case of finished or partly finished goods in the hands of the manufacturer, the cost of production is the measure of damage, exclusive of profits and without any addition to the cost for interest on capital employed either in plant or machinery.

**Goods in course of manufacture.**

One important respect in which the conditions of fire insurance differ from those in marine insurance is in regard

Partial loss.

Fire insurance differs from marine.

to Partial loss. Thus, if in the case of a factory consisting of one building, constituting one "risk" worth £10,000, the owner chooses to insure it only for £8000, and if part of the factory be burnt to the extent of £8000, the insurer can, according to the General English practice, recover that sum, while in marine insurance if only 8-10ths of the total value had been covered, only 8-10ths of the partial loss would be paid.

Colonial and foreign losses.

This rule of English fire offices extends also to property in the Colonies insured by them, but as in most Foreign countries the condition just described as usual in marine insurance prevails for fire risks also, English fire offices generally adopt it in the policies they issue in such countries.

Each building deemed a separate risk.

The English practice of "specific assurance," as it is called, does not, however, apply when several buildings are insured together in one sum. When the property lies in more places than one, so as to form a plurality of risks, it is required either that a distinct sum shall be insured upon the property contained in every separate building or place, or that the assurance shall be subject to the condition of average, or "average clause" as it is termed.*

Example of separate buildings.

For instance, if a factory consisting of two or more separate blocks of buildings be insured in one sum for £5000, and if one block be burnt, only the proportionate value which this one building bore to the whole is recoverable, even though its value may be £5000. Were it otherwise, two or more blocks of buildings might be insured for the premium of one, on the presumption that the risk was remote of more than one being burnt at the same time.

Fireproof divisions separate the risk.

In this respect rooms or workshops separated by fireproof doors in the manner prescribed by the Building Acts for structures of a certain size are deemed separate buildings

* See 'The Law of Fire Insurance,' by Charles John Bunyon, M.A., Barrister-at-Law. London: Charles and Edwin Layton.

and must be separately insured. There are also special rules in this respect for merchandise stored in public warehouses or on wharfs during transit.

**Alterations in factory affect the insurance**

It is desirable for the foregoing reasons that any considerable addition to or redistribution of the plant in different workshops should be notified to the insurance office, even if the value is still within the amount of the policy. If such alterations have in any way increased the risks of fire, either by circumstances inherent in the factory itself, or by contiguity to other buildings, then the neglect of such intimation may imperil the claim for compensation.

**Conformity to conditions.**

Although equitable treatment may be reckoned on by those who are themselves acting fairly, even if the information they have furnished does not fully come up to the conditions imposed by the insurance office, yet in many cases difficulties which might have been avoided arise from an insufficient conformity to such conditions.

**Insurance offices reserve option of reinstatement.**

Although, as has been said, Indemnity for what has been destroyed is alone recoverable, and Reinstatement cannot be claimed, the insurance offices always reserve the option of reinstating instead of making a money payment if they deem the estimate of loss to be excessive.

**Consequential losses are not insurable.**

**Contract values or profits not insurable.**

Consequential damage for losses by fire cannot be insured in English fire offices, though some of the underwriters at Lloyd's, who undertake fire risks arising in connection with marine risks, will occasionally insure such losses. Such, for instance, are the loss of time and profit which a fire may cause, and in the same category would be the contract value of, or the expected profit on, goods which are ready or in course of preparation for delivery. If the insurer can show that he was about to receive a certain sum for goods which have been damaged or consumed, such a fact, while it may assist in arriving at the true value, will not be accepted as the basis of a claim.

**Losses appraised at current value.** The current wholesale value must be appraised, and it may be more or less than the contract price.

The leading principle of all fire insurance offices is to afford no opportunity for the insured to derive profit from a fire, and it is for this reason that profits on goods and consequential damages, which are difficult to appraise, are excluded.

**Rent may be insured** But to the implied rule, that only tangible losses are insurable, there is the exception of Rent, which as having a precise value that may be defined and that is not so liable as other indirect loss to be varied after the policy has been issued, is insurable. A landlord may insure the rent he would lose by reason of a fire; an occupier may insure the rent which, after a fire, may continue to be payable under the terms of a lease; and an occupier who owns his factory may insure the rent which he might have to pay for the use of another factory during the reinstatement of the one destroyed or damaged. But, a maximum of one year's rent is generally prescribed, and, as in the case of direct loss by fire, whatever amount for rent may have been insured, the compensation is limited to the amount actually lost. **if stated in the policy.** Of course when it is desired to insure rent this must be specifically stated in the policy.

# CHAPTER XII.

## THE RATEABLE VALUE OF FACTORIES.

FACTORIES are rated for the Relief of the Poor on their Net annual Value. To arrive at this value, the gross Rent that a tenant would pay is ascertained or estimated, and a certain proportion of it is deducted for the cost of repairs, maintenance, fire insurance, and other charges which, taking an average of years, would have to be provided for before an annual net profit can be reckoned.

**Rateable value, how arrived at.**

The proportion of the gross rent which should be so deducted must of course vary with the nature of the property and the burdens upon it. In the case of land, the net value may approach very nearly to the gross rental; in the case of buildings, if they are old, and the cost of repairs and maintenance heavy, the deduction should be greater than with new and well-constructed buildings. But even in the latter case, eventual rebuilding must be held in view, and a depreciation rate or reserve allowed for which will maintain or replace the net income.

**Deductions from gross value.**

The principle of assessment on the net rental value is generally easy of application when, as in the case of a dwelling-house, the property is let to a yearly tenant, whose rent, confirmed by that paid for similar houses in the locality, forms a basis of calculation. The actual rent paid by a tenant is not, however, always conclusive, because it may happen that, owing to special circumstances, such rent is more or less than that which would be paid under ordinary conditions. Thus, there may be obligations on

**Assessment based on actual rent.**

**Rent not always a fair basis.**

the tenant in regard to repairs or reinstatement, which may make the rent more nearly approach the net annual value than is usual, or the tenant may be occupying under an old lease at a rent much below the current value. On the other hand, there may be certain privileges or indirect advantages in connection with the property which may induce a particular tenant to pay more than the property would fetch if let upon its own merits.

**Difficulties in rating of factories.**

Two main questions, sometimes involving considerable difficulty, have arisen in estimating the rateable value of Factories. One, where the factory, the fixtures and the plant belong to the Occupier and there is no separate sum charged for Rent, and where therefore the rental value has to be estimated; and the second, where it has to be determined which, if any, of the fixtures and plant are to be included in the "net rental" valuation.

*See page* 107.

**Tenant's profits not rateable.**

In regard to the first of these suppositions: where there is no tenant and therefore no actual rent paid, it is necessary to estimate what annual sum a tenant would be willing to pay for the use of the factory in question. The profits of the tenant earned by his own skill and capital are not rateable, and it must be considered merely what rent a tenant who bore the general risks of the business would pay. In estimating this, the cost of the factory and of similar factories, and the interest on the capital invested in them, are important aids to the calculation, but they are not conclusive. Owing to alterations in the trade in question, or in the method and cost of building factories engaged in such trades, or from local causes, the value of the factory may have fallen, and the rent which a tenant would be willing to pay may be less than the interest usual on building investments of a similar class. Or the reverse may be the case. Since the factory was built, its value may have risen, either through a general rise in the value of land in the locality, or from an increase in the cost of building such factories, or from local or trade causes

**The cost of factories not a conclusive basis.**

**Growth of value.**

which have increased the profits derivable from such factories, and have increased therefore the rent which an occupier would be willing to pay for the opportunity of earning such profit.

**Factories not earning a direct profit.**

The difficulty of arriving at a rental value where there is no tenant and no rent to be paid, is increased where the factory is carried on as part of a larger undertaking, and with no direct profit arising from it. Such is the case in Government or municipal workshops, or those attached to water or gas supply undertakings, where the value of the workshops is only a portion of the larger capital invested in street mains and other property; or in the case of railway workshops, where locomotives and wagons are repaired for use on the railway. The difficulty is sometimes solved by the rating authorities agreeing with the occupiers to accept as the rating value an agreed interest on the capital shown to have been invested in the workshops; but in the event of difference, the method reefrred to above has to be adopted of estimating what an imaginary tenant would pay, giving full consideration to the orginal cost and the rate of interest that would be remunerative as rental.

**Railway workshops.** *See page* 3.

**Assessment based on capital value.** *See page* 116.

**Rateability of machinery and plant.**

In regard to the second point previously referred to, of how far Machinery and Plant should be included in the Rateable value, considerable changes have from time to time taken place in the application of the rules laid down for the rateability of machinery. It has sometimes been sought to exclude trade fixtures from rateability. Although it is clear on the highest authority that chattels as such are not rateable, yet trade fixtures are in general clearly to be rated. In a well-known text-book * on the subjcct it is stated,—

**Trade fixtures.** *See page* 118.

"That they are part of the freehold and would pass under a mortgage, and though in the case of a factory a tenant is allowed to

* See 'A Practical Treatise on the Law of Rating,' by Edward James Castle, Barrister-at-Law. 1879. London: Stevens and Sons.

**Fixtures removable by tenant.**

remove them during his term, it is not in the same way as he might remove his furniture from a house, but only because the Courts were induced to relax the strictness of the old rules of law in order that the commercial interests of the country might be enhanced by the encouragement given to a tenant to employ his capital in making improvements for carrying on trade from the certainty of having the benefit of the expenditure secured to him at the end of his term."

**Plant, as tenant's fixtures, not rateable.**

It became usual in many parts of the country, apparently on the supposition that machines and plant removable as above by the tenant were not landlord's fixtures, to include in the rateable value only those fixtures which by the narrower view of the law, or by usage, clearly pertained to the freehold. Therefore, while boilers, furnaces, steam-engines, lines of shafting, and other apparatus which were deemed permanent were included, machines which were attached only by their own weight, or were only steadied by bolts, or which could easily be removed by a tenant without damage to the premises, were excluded from the rateable valve. In fact, much the same separation into classes prevailed as is prescribed in the Bills of Sale Act, passed for an entirely different purpose.

**Engines and boilers rateable.**

**Bills of Sale Act.** *See page* 120.

But, although as a matter of usage this method of classification became established in certain districts and produced, in the case of particular trades, the same result as would a strict interpretation of the law, the principle of excluding machinery was not always upheld in cases were disputes came before the Courts. The diversity of practice arose mainly from the fact that the valuation is in the first instance in the hands of local overseers or parochial assessment committees, who apply in different ways rules that had become established for other kinds of property. Such local valuations, however, take effect, and are followed as precedents in the district, unless appealed against in the superior courts of law. Appeals have sometimes been made by occupiers who

**Machinery not always excluded.**

**Diversity of practice.**

**Appeals to the superior courts.**

deem themselves too heavily rated, but as often by those who consider that their neighbours are insufficiently rated. It is in the decisions of the judges on these appeal cases, rather than in any statutes easy to be understood, that the law on the subject is to be found.

**Law to be found in judges' decisions.**

Some of the earlier cases were appeals from assessments, where the plant omitted was of a kind generally included even when removable fixtures are excluded. Thus in the case* of the Phœnix Gas Company, in 1866, it was held that the retorts, purifiers, gas-holders, steam-engines, and boilers, were to be taken into account in assessing the rateable value, because they were fixtures which added permanently to the value of the premises; and that also the mains in the public streets were rateable; but that the meters which were the property of the company in the private houses of the consumers were not rateable, because they were not indispensable to the manufacture of gas, for which purpose the works were established.

**Case of the Phœnix Gas Co**

It still appeared, and was so acted on in many parts of the country, as if machinery of a kind more easily removable should be excluded, and this was apparently confirmed in the case of the Halstead silk factory,† where it was held by the Court of Queen's Bench, on appeal in 1867, that while the value of the steam-engines, boilers, and shafting must be included in the assessment, the looms and other machines merely screwed to the floor were not to be included. In this case the machines were treated as the furnishing of a mill, which could be easily removed. The judge said, "These machines are common things in Lancashire. They are carried from one manufactory to another, and can be removed from one room to another. They are not so

**Case of the Halstead silk mill.**

**Looms not rateable.**

*See page* 120.

**Because not permanently fixed.**

* *Regina* v. *The Inhabitants of the Parish of Lee*, Law Reports, 1, Q. Bench Cases, 241.

† *Regina* v. *Overseers of Halstead.* The Justice of the Peace, February 22, 1868.

permanently fixed to the building as in the case of the gas-works."

This decision had the effect of confirming the system which prevailed in many districts in the assessment of all kinds of manufactories, but in the following year what appeared to be a stricter interpretation of the law again opened up the question of rateability. The Overseers of Bishopwearmouth, in a new assessment of the premises of Messrs. Laing, the shipbuilders, included in the valuation not only the steam-engines, steam-hammers, boilers, and shafting, but also the lathes and machines for planing, drilling, punching and riveting; and against this assessment Messrs. Laing appealed to the Court of Queen's Bench, where the assessment on this wider basis was confirmed.* Chief Justice Cockburn, in his judgment stated, "It appears to us, after having carefully considered the character of the machinery in question, that the whole of it, though some of it may be capable of being removed without injury to itself or to the freehold, is essentially necessary to the shipbuilding business to which the appellants' premises are devoted, and must be taken to be intended to remain permanently attached to them so long as the premises are applied to their present purpose."

**Case of Laing, shipbuilder.**

**Machine tools held to be rateable.**

This case† attracted much attention, and as an authoritative declaration of the law was adopted in some other localities. But the decision is generally considered to have gone too far; if logically applied to factories in general, it might be held to include all machines; and the less rigid interpretation of the law which includes only undoubted

**Laing's case not generally approved.**

* *Laing* v. *Overseers of Bishopwearmouth*, Law Reports, 3, Q. Bench Div., p. 299.

† Full particulars of this and previous cases are given in a book entitled 'Local Taxation and the Rating of Machinery,' by T. F. Hedley, of Sunderland (Knight and Co., Fleet Street, London), who supports the decision in the Laing case. The opposite view is maintained by James Pott, jun., of Sunderland, in a pamphlet 'Remarks on the Assessment of Machinery,' published by E. and F. N. Spon, London.

fixtures in the rateable value continued to be generally applied. *See page* 113. **Bill of 1893.**

In comparing the decision with that in the Halstead case, the question arises as to where the line is to be drawn in including plant and machinery in the rateable value of a factory, because some of it may be as easily removable as is the furniture of a dwelling-house. An operative watch-maker would remove his lathe if the tenancy of his house and workshop expires; a Nottingham lace-maker removes his loom from the workshop where he rents floor-space and power; and the looms are, therefore, not rated.

**As tending to make all tools rateable.**

*See page* 89.

The question in regard to machines and machine-tools seems, therefore, to be this*—Would they be landlord's or tenant's fixtures in an occupation from year to year? Are they of such a perishable nature as not to outlast a yearly tenancy? Are they of a kind which so quickly wear out that a yearly tenant would find it worth while to attach them to the building? Would structural alterations be required to allow the machinery to be attached to the premises? and other circumstances which would in an ordinary yearly tenancy determine whether the machinery should be supplied by the landlord or tenant.

**The real question as to fixtures.**

It is not necessary to consider whether a tenant would as a matter of fact remove his machinery and plant, but whether by usage, and as appropriate to the trade in question, he would have the right to remove them or sell them to a new tenant. There are many kinds of house fixtures, such as gas-fittings, and blinds, which, though the property of a tenant, are gencrally left behind and sold to the incoming tenant. Still, as tenant's fixtures they would be excluded from the rateable value, and the machine-tools of an engineer are generally regarded in this light, notwithstanding the decision in the Laing case. But according to this decision, if a factory were so constructed as to be useful

**Machines removable by tenant.**

**Engineer's tools deemed to be removable.**

* E. J. Castle. See footnote, p. 107.

for no other purpose than that for which the machinery and plant had been fitted to it, such a circumstance would affect the decision as to the rateability of the plant.

It is to be noticed that in the Laing case the judges did not investigate the facts, but merely decided on facts presented to them; and in the case it was stated that the machines were intended to be permanently used.

**Scotch decision.**

Although there is no difference between Scotch and English law in this respect, a different decision which tended to uphold the practice was given in 1887 in the case of the workshops of the North British Railway at Cowlairs.* In this case it was held that unless the machinery was so attached that it could not be removed without destruction to itself or the building it was not rateable.

It will be seen that though certain principles of law have been declared by the judges, no actual enumeration of plant or machinery has been made. The principle having been agreed upon, the knowledge of engineers or others acquainted with the necessities and usage of particular trades is required to apply the rules to the factory whose rateability is in question.

**Uniformity of rating system desirable.**

It is desirable that the question should be set at rest either by a case more carefully drawn up and presented than the Laing case, and representative of the leading industries of the country, or, if necessary, by fresh legislation on the subject. So long as each local authority is allowed to settle the matter, as apparently they may do in the absence of an appeal, manufacturers in one district may be assessed much more heavily than those in another district with whom they compete; and even in the same town manufacturers of one class, such as engineers, to whom the

* Court of Session, Bill Chamber, September 26, 1887, before Lord Fraser. *The North British Railway Company* v. *The Assessor of Railways and Canals in Scotland.*

Laing case more immediately applies, may contribute a larger share to the relief of the poor than do those of another class, such as those engaged in the textile trades, who are equally employers of labour.

**Attempts to arrive at uniformity.**

The inconveniences arising from the different interpretations and applications of the law became so serious, that on several occasions subsequent to 1885 Bills were introduced into Parliament for settling the question. The purport of the Bills was not the formulating of any new views, but rather a declaration that the old usage was the right one, namely that only landlords' fixtures were rateable.

**Bills in Parliament.**

The Bills failed to pass into law, at first rather for want of time than from opposition, which arose principally from the representatives of agricultural districts who feared that the burdens on land might be increased if those on manufactories were lightened. But in 1890–1 some representatives of urban constituencies also opposed the Bill on the ground that the rates of shopkeepers and private residents, who had no apparent interest in manufactories would suffer if factories were relieved by the proposed legislation.

**Bill of 1893.**

In the Session of 1893 there was introduced into the House of Commons "A Bill to amend the Law relating to the rating of hereditaments containing machinery.

"Whereas questions have from time to time arisen as to how far machinery is to be taken into consideration in estimating the rateable value of the premises in which any trade, business, or manufacture is carried on, and it is expedient to amend the law relating thereto:

"Be it therefore enacted by the Queen's most Excellent Majesty, by and with the advice and consent of the Lords Spiritual and Temporal, and Commons, in this present Parliament assembled, and by the authority of the same, as follows:—

"1. From and after the *passing of this Act*, in estimating for the purpose of any valuation list, or poor or other local rate, the gross estimated rental or rateable value of any hereditament occupied for any trade, business, or manufacturing purposes, any increased value arising from machines, tools or appliances which are not fixed or are only so fixed that they can be removed from their place without necessitating the removal of any part of the said hereditament shall be excluded.

"Provided that the gross annual value of any such hereditament shall be estimated at not less than the sum at which it might reasonably be expected to let for the purpose for which it is used on a tenancy from year to year void of the machines, tools, and appliances which it might reasonably be expected would be supplied by the tenant, if the tenant paid all the usual tenants' rates and taxes and tithe rentcharge (if any), and if the landlord undertook to bear the cost of the repairs and insurance and the other expenses (if any) necessary to maintain the said hereditament in a state to command such rent.

"Provided also that the terms machines, tools, and appliances for the purposes of this Act shall not apply to any machinery, machine, or plant used in or on the hereditament for producing or transmitting first motive power, or for heating or lighting the said hereditament.

"2. Nothing in this Act contained shall apply to the rating of waterworks or gasworks.

"3. This Act shall not apply to Scotland or Ireland.

"4. This Act may be cited as the Rating of Machinery Act, 1893."

To the above bill an amendment was moved—Clause 1, at end add "and provided further that such machinery, machine or plant, used for producing or transmitting first motive power shall not be assessed for the purpose of rating at less than fifty pounds for each nominal horse-power, unless in any particular case there shall be laid before the rating authority reasons which in their judgment are sufficient to warrant them in adopting a lower assessment.

An amendment was also moved to leave out Clause 2.

**Rateable value of machinery how arrived at.**

Assuming that machinery is to be rated, the valuation should be made on the same principle as for buildings, but it is almost always necessary to allow a wider margin between gross and net value. The cost of repairs and renewals is generally greater than with buildings, for the deterioration is more rapid, and assuming a tenant who pays rent for the use of such plant, but who had not the burden of reinstatement, the landlord would have to apply a considerable proportion of the gross rental to such charges. Therefore, to take the case of an engineering factory or steel works, while one-sixth might be a sufficient allowance from the gross annual value of buildings, one-fourth or even more might have to be allowed from the machinery to arrive at the net rental value.

**Gross and net rental value.**

**Broad rules for rating**

In districts where there are many factories engaged in the same industry, the assessment is sometimes made according to certain broad rules, by which a minute investtigation of every case is avoided. Thus, in some parts of Lancashire the annual rateable value of cotton-spinning factories will be reckoned at so much per spindle (even though the spindles themselves are not included in the value), on the assumption that the number of spindles determines with sufficient accuracy the size of the mill and its value to a tenant. Again, in the engineering trades, the engines, boilers, and shafting, or whatever in the particular district is included in the rateable value, is assessed broadly at so much per horse-power.* This, though a convenient method, may be applied too widely, and sometimes presses unduly on the older factories. Thus, in a modern cotton-mill, arranged after an improved method, the

**not always applicable.**

* See p. 114. Amendment to Bill of 1893.

same number of looms or spindles as in an older mill may afford a greater or more valuable output, and the rental and rateable values are, therefore, greater than in an older mill; or, in an engineering factory, there may have been a large capital outlay in improved steam-engines which consume a minimum of fuel. An engine of 100 horse-power which consumes only 2 lbs. of coal per horse-power per hour has obviously a higher rental value than one of similar power which consumes 4 lbs. per horse-power.

**Value of engines according to power.**

**Altered values.** *See page* 58.
**Deterioration.** *See page* 3.

*See page* 58.

An increase or decrease in the rental and rateable value owing to additions or deterioration has sometimes to be considered. In an old factory, if the buildings and plant have been fairly maintained, the annual value to a tenant may be undiminished even though the capital value to the proprietor may have decreased. But if the plant has become old-fashioned, or be no longer capable of producing so good or so much work as formerly, the rental value is obviously less, and an abatement may be claimed.

**Burden of rates equally allotted.**

**Railway companies unduly rated.**

On the one hand, it is due to the neighbouring proprietors of a district who are properly assessed, that owners of factories shall contribute their full share to the public burdens; and on the other hand, care is necessary to prevent overcharge to factory owners, and especially to large corporations like railway companies, whose shareholders are widely spread and who do not always meet with the same consideration from the local authorities as do private owners.

**Rating based on capital value.** *See page* 107.

In the case of workshops belonging to railways and other corporations, where no direct profit is earned and where an agreed rate of interest on the capital outlay is accepted as a fair rateable value, the ordinary rules have to be observed in discriminating between a gross and net rental. Thus, if 5 per cent. on buildings be agreed upon as a fair rateable value, this would represent 6 or 7 per cent.

as a gross rental from a tenant; and if much plant or machinery were included, although a rent to be remunerative might have to be 10 per cent., the net or rateable value might still be 5 per cent. If the land be taken separately, interest at 4 per cent. on the capital outlay is usual as an annual rateable value.

## CHAPTER XIII.

### TRADE FIXTURES—BILLS OF SALE—DEBENTURES.

**Landlord's and Tenant's fixtures.**

IN the preceding chapter, the question of Fixtures has been dealt with in regard to the rateable value of factories. Similar questions may arise between Landlord and Tenant, or between Freeholder and Occupier, or in the sale or transfer of a factory; for, although there are certain kinds of factory plant which are clearly the personal chattels of the tenant, and others which as clearly pertain to the freehold, there are often in or about a factory appliances or structures which cannot readily be placed in either category.

**Fixtures attached to the land.**

*See page* 108.

Fixtures attached to the land either directly or indirectly become part of the freehold, but as has already been shown it is generally held by a relaxation of the law in this respect that many of the additions made for the purposes of trade may be removed by the tenant during his term. But the mode of attachment is an important element in the case, as well also as the exact purpose. Thus a boiler firmly built into brickwork, or a steam-engine on massive foundations, would be considered as permanent fixtures, while a machine placed without fastenings and held in position merely by its own weight, or one fastened by screws, allowing of removal without damage to the structure, do not generally become part of the freehold.

**Steam boilers and engines.**

**Machines.**

**Disputes avoided by agreements beforehand.**

Disputes may, however, be best avoided by making precise stipulations in the lease or other agreement. A tenant may anticipate the necessity or desirability of making additions, which, in the absence of an agreement to the contrary, might be claimed as landlord's fixtures, and he will, if possible, stipulate that he may remove them at the end of his term, if damage to the ground and buildings be avoided or made good, the option being sometimes left to the landlord to retain such fixtures on paying their value. Where one of several partners in a factory is the freeholder, the ultimate right to the fixtures and plant which have been bought or added at the expense of the firm should be clearly declared in the partnership deed or agreement of tenancy. Where the additions or improvements so relate to the land or buildings that they cannot easily be removed, compensation, and not removal, may alone be feasible; but for such additions the consent of the landlord is generally necessary.

**Where one partner owns the freehold.**

The classification given in Clause 5 of the Bills of Sale Act, though made for a different purpose and not binding for any other, indicates very nearly the kind of distinction which prevails in the absence of agreement to the contrary, and this same classification follows very nearly on the lines which have been adopted in many districts as the basis of valuation for purposes of rating.

**Classification as in Bills of Sale Act.**

*See page* 120.

*See page* 108.

There is another aspect of this question of fixtures directly affecting the owners or occupiers of factories, which though it has been much simplified by legislation, often gives cause for dispute, namely, the respective rights of Mortgagees and unsecured Creditors against the property in "trade machinery" of a Debtor.

**Creditors and Mortgagees.**

Until the year 1878, a judgment creditor, or the general creditors of an insolvent estate, often found, on attempting to realise the property of a debtor, that much of the plant and machinery which they had looked upon as available in case of need for payment of their debt had been already assigned. Thus, while by examining public registers or the lists issued by trade protection societies, traders are kept aware of assignments by Bills of Sale, it was

**Factory plant assigned.**

Uncertainty of the law.

repeatedly found from the uncertainty of the law in regard to fixtures, or by the ingenious application or perversion of the law, or from the various constructions put upon the law by different judges in the varying circumstances that arose, that machinery and plant could be secretly pledged or assigned to certain persons, to the exclusion of all other creditors. The opportunities thus afforded for fraudulent preference and for collusion between a debtor and favoured creditors, were greatly limited by the "Bills of Sale Act, 1878," entitled—"An Act to consolidate and amend the law for preventing frauds upon creditors by secret Bills of Sale of personal chattels." By this Act, no assignment of trade machinery can be made except by a registered bill of sale, and regarding these, the Act declares in section 5:—

Fraudulent preference.

Bills of Sale Act of 1878.

"5. From and after the commencement of this Act trade machinery shall, for the purposes of this Act, be deemed to be personal chattels, and any mode of disposition of trade machinery by the owner thereof which would be a bill of sale as to any other personal chattels shall be deemed to be a bill of sale within the meaning of this Act.

"For the purposes of this Act—

Trade machinery defined.

'Trade machinery' means the machinery used in or attached to any factory or workshop;

1st. Exclusive of the fixed motive-powers, such as the water-wheels and steam-engines, and the steam-boilers, donkey engines, and other fixed appurtenances of the said motive-powers; and,

Motive powers and shafting excepted.

2nd. Exclusive of the fixed power machinery, such as the shafts, wheels, drums, and their fixed appurtenances, which transmit the action of the motive-powers to the other machinery, fixed and loose; and,

3rd. Exclusive of the pipes for steam, gas, and water in the factory or workshop.

The machinery or effects excluded by this section from the definition of trade machinery shall not be deemed to be personal chattels within the meaning of this Act.

Factory or workshop defined.

'Factory or workshop' means any premises on which any manual labour is exercised by way of trade, or for purposes of gain, in or incidental to the following purposes or any of them; that is to say,

(*a.*) In or incidental to the making any article or part of an article ; or
(*b.*) In or incidental to the altering, repairing, ornamenting, finishing, of any article ; or
(*c.*) In or incidental to the adapting for sale any article."

It will be seen from the above clauses that steam-engines, boilers, shafting and other fixtures are excluded, but it must not be assumed that they necessarily pass with the freehold. In the absence of a precise agreement between the parties, the kind, purpose, and mode of attachment would have to be considered ; as also, in regard to a mortgage, would its terms and all the surrounding circumstances. On the other hand, while for the particular purposes of the Bills of Sale Act, and to prevent frauds upon creditors, trade machinery is deemed to be personal chattels, it does not follow that they are so for all intents and purposes, as has already been seen in the case of rateable value. Nor would the classification of the Bills of Sale Act necessarily apply between mortgagor and mortgagee where there were no other creditors. Factory plant is of such various kinds, and is connected to the ground in so many ways that it is difficult to lay down any precise rules for general application.

**Classification of trade fixtures**

**limited in application.**

*See page* 111.

In 1882 was passed the "Bills of Sale (1878) Amendment Act," which does not affect the main principles of the original Act, but amongst other amendments adds in sections 4, 14, and 17, the following :—

**Bills of Sale Amendment Act of 1882.**

"4. Every bill of sale shall have annexed thereto or written thereon a schedule containing an inventory of the personal chattels comprised in the bill of sale ; and such bill of sale, save as hereinafter mentioned, shall have effect only in respect of the personal chattels specifically described in the said schedule ; and shall be void, except as against the grantor, in respect of any personal chattels not so specifically described."

**Schedule necessary.**

"14. A bill of sale to which this Act applies shall be no protection in respect of personal chattels included in such bill of sale which but for such bill of sale would have been liable to distress under a warrant for the recovery of taxes and poor and other parochial rates."

**Rent and taxes have precedence.**

**Debentures**

"17. Nothing in this Act shall apply to any debentures issued by any mortgage, loan, or other incorporated company, and secured upon the capital stock or goods, chattels, and effects of such company."

It will be seen from these clauses that taxes and rates take precedence, as also does rent, of claims under a bill of sale.

There is the marked difference between Debentures and Bills of Sales, so far as general or outside creditors are concerned, that the debentures are not filed or registered in a public office where any one can inspect them, and are not therefore published in the weekly lists that are issued by private trade protection societies. But, under the Companies' Act of 1862, debentures, to be valid, must be registered in the books of the company that issues them; the omission of such registration renders the directors personally liable; and all persons concerned can claim to examine the register on payment of a fee of one shilling. Although debenture assignments are not registered in a public office like bills of sale, a list of shareholders, with the amount of share capital paid up and uncalled has to be filed every year at the Registry Office in London, and can be inspected by any one on payment of a fee of one shilling.

**must be registered.**

In the case of debentures issued by any incorporated manufacturing company, the extent to which the security mortgaged includes machinery and plant has to be carefully considered by all concerned. A debenture is supposed generally to be a form of mortgage, but the word is applied to securities of very different kinds. Without a knowledge of the exact terms of a debenture it must not be assumed that it constitutes a first charge or security. Debentures are in England issuable by most companies, whether "limited" or not, and in many the powers in this respect are defined and restricted by general or special Acts of Parliament.

**Debentures vary.**

**Restricted by Acts of Parliament.**

Some debentures merely acknowledge indebtedness;

others are really only Preference Shares, and in regard to the capital or assets of the company which issues the debentures, though the holders might take precedence of ordinary shareholders in any winding up, they would rank only with other and unsecured creditors.

**Some debentures only preference shares.**

In most railways, and the rule is generally adopted by other well-constituted joint-stock companies, the amount of the debentures is limited to a certain proportion, generally one-third of the paid-up share capital, the object being to give the debenture holders an assurance of the value of their security. Where a moderate proportion of this sort is ignored, and sometimes even when it is observed, the money raised by debentures may have formed the only beneficial expenditure and afford the only assets. American railway and other bonds are often of this kind.

**Debentures limited in amount.**

Some debentures mortgage the property of a company in a way which affects greatly the security of the general creditors, and this in regard to the trade fixtures. Such debentures are often very sweeping in their application, all the material assets of the company being assigned to trustees for the benefit of the debenture holder, the goodwill and in some cases even the uncalled part of the share capital being included in the assignment. Such debentures may hamper greatly the management of a manufacturing company, for the directors may be restrained from selling, exchanging, removing, or otherwise dealing advantageously with the plant of the factory. Care and skill are necessary in the framing of a debenture to give the maximum security to the debenture holders, with the minimum of restriction on the management.

**Trade fixtures mortgaged.**

**All assets included.**

The Companies' Act of 1862 prescribes that in the register of debentures must be given a description of what is included in the mortgage, this description, so far as the protection of general creditors is concerned, being the equivalent of a schedule attached to a bill of sale.

**Debentures must be registered and inventory added.**

## CHAPTER XIV.

### THE LOCALITY OF FACTORIES.

*See pages* 75, 83, 90.

**Locality of a factory affects its value.**

In a previous chapter reference was made to the circumstances of Locality, which, apart from any general estimate of buildings and plant, go to determine the value of a factory for a particular trade. These circumstances should have been considered in the first establishment of the undertaking, but they are obviously an important factor in estimating value at a change of ownership. What was but conjecture or calculation before the factory was built, will now have been tested by actual experience.

**Conditions of value vary for different trades.**

It is as impossible as it would be presumptuous to set up rules for guidance in the infinite number of circumstances and combinations that present themselves, or to say which are the conditions in regard to locality and site which must determine value; and it is only attempted to enumerate some of the leading points that should be considered. It is always dangerous to follow precedent unless the circumstances are exactly similar; and what may have proved of the first importance in one branch of trade, or at a particular period, may be of secondary or no importance in another case. It is impossible to combine all advantages in any one factory; care should be exercised therefore in observing due proportion in estimating their value.

**Chief incidents of locality.**

The choice of locality * depends mainly on the contiguity to Material, on the cost of Transport, on the abundance of Labour, and on contiguity to the Consumer.

* See 'Aid-book to Engineering Enterprise,' by the same author, described at the end of this volume.

**Taxation.**

Taxation and other public burdens have also to be considered; for these vary in different localities, and in some cases it is cheaper to establish a factory outside a certain district or town.

**Contiguity to materials.**

The importance of contiguity to suitable materials depends on their weight or bulk, on the cost of carriage, and the proportion which this bears to the whole cost of production. In trades where the cost of material bears a small proportion to the total expenses of production, distance may matter little; for instance, a maker of cutlery and firearms is not—other circumstances being favourable—weighted much even if the iron and steel are brought from a considerable distance.

**Cost of carriage sometimes unimportant.**

A locality near the material might be chosen where the latter was much heavier than the finished products, while if the products were also heavy, contiguity to the consumer or to a port of shipment might determine the choice. The effect which transport and storage may have on the quality of the material or finished goods has also to be considered.

**Expenses of carriage.**

The cost of Carriage to the port often amounts to as much as, or more than, the freight by sea to a distant country; and this circumstance, of course, is of increased importance for those commodities in which the expense of carriage bears a considerable proportion to their total selling price. In England the favourable situation of the coal and iron mines near to the sea allows manufactories to be established with both the above advantages, but nearness to a port is not always best for an inland trade.

**Ports where materials arrive.**

Factories are often established in the neighbourhood of ports at which the materials of manufacture arrive, or the factories having been established, the materials come there; thus, for example, there are seed-crushing mills at Hull, jute factories at Dundee, and cotton mills in Lancashire. But whether the factories follow the cargo, or the cargo the factories, Cheap freights inward depend upon the vessels obtaining return cargo, and when this is wanting the materials are burdened with higher freights. There are many instances of trade having left a particular district for reasons of this kind; and the risk is increased where the commerce of a port depends upon customs tariffs liable to alteration.

**Customs tariffs.**

**Contiguity to a port.**

While, however, the contiguity to a port may be advantageous where the goods are heavy, and may more than compensate for drawbacks which the locality may have in other respects, the choice and value of any particular port depend on various considerations. Where the goods are shipped in large quantities, as is often the case with coals, iron, or railway material, a vessel may be sent to the nearest port to fetch the cargo instead of the cargo being sent to a port which suits the vessel. But even where the goods offered are not sufficient to fill a vessel, they may be enough to induce a shipowner to send his vessel to call at a particular port to fetch them, to complete a cargo commenced or finished elsewhere.

**Suitability of a port, how determined.**

A port or harbour must be suitable for the particular trade and for the vessels which go to the foreign countries whose commerce is desired. Thus there must be sufficient draught of water, safe navigation, railway communications, facilities for wharfage and handling of goods, and moderate dues. In regard to the export of manufactured goods there must be inducements for vessels to enter. Such inducement may be in the abundance and variety of goods to be exported, but if it be a brisk import trade which brings vessels to the port, it may be an advantage to a manufactory that its products are alone available for outward cargo; as, in the absence of competing cargo, low rates of freight outward may be obtained.

Some trades indeed depend entirely on cheap rates of freight, only rendered possible by the necessities of the shipowner. Thus, cement, iron, and other rough goods

**Ballast cargo.**

are carried from London to New York at rates of from 4*s*. to 8*s*. per ton, because ballast cargo is wanted and the American tariff limits the shipment of general merchandise. So also iron ore is shipped at Lisbon at 3*s*. per ton, and brimstone from Sicily at 10*s*. per ton to the United States. The real cost of freight is in these cases partly paid by the shippers of light goods westward, but mainly by the shipper of produce from America, who must pay enough to remunerate the shipowner for the double voyage. On the other hand, if there is not much inward trade, then an abundance of outward cargo may be necessary to attract vessels. Therefore, although vessels to any foreign country may sail indifferently from any British port, it has become the custom, either because of the exigencies of the homeward trade, or because certain harbours are suitable for the vessels in question, or for other economical reasons, that particular trades or destinations are associated with particular ports of departure, and factories connected with these trades are established in the vicinity.

**Customary ports.**

Perhaps there is no better instance anywhere of the localisation of a trade than that of the manufacture of Portland cement in the neighbourhood of London, on the rivers Thames and Medway. The chalk and clay from which the cement is made are found close together, on or near the river bank, and yet quite separate, so that the proper proportions can be exactly measured; the coke from the large gas-works of London, also on the river-side, affords a cheap and plentiful supply of suitable fuel; and the situation of the factories allows the cement to be loaded into barges, coasting vessels, and export ships at a trifling expense. Moreover, as vessels leave London for almost all foreign ports, the cement as weight or ballast cargo has the advantage of very low freights.

**Trade localised.**

**Example of Portland cement.**

Inland Water-carriage affords many advantages, as goods once embarked may be carried long distances at a much

**Inland water-carriage.**

less cost than by road or railway; and in case of bulky, heavy, or fragile goods the risks of carriage are generally less. For, however much competition or other causes may reduce rates of railway freight, the bare cost of haulage must at least be paid. Canals and navigable rivers can always compete with railways in the cheapness of carriage, except when a very prompt delivery is of great importance.

**Canal carriage.**

The advantages of canal carriage are, however, often neutralised by artificial restrictions, as for instance, when they are controlled by the railway companies.

**Cartage expensive for heavy goods.**

Cartage is a serious item of expense in some trades, and may be onerous enough, if competition arises with other factories more favourably situated in this regard, to stop the business, or to absorb nearly all of what without the cartage would be a remunerative profit. Thus, an iron foundry at the top of a hill, or at a distance from a railway station, is heavily burdened in regard to the cartage of pig-iron, coal, sand, and castings. Even a small distance may render necessary the keeping of horses and carters, as well as an expense of loading and unloading, which would be avoided if the factory were situated on a railway siding or canal.

**Horses.**

*See page* 48.

**Railway sidings.**

Sometimes the expense lies not in constant cartage but in the occasional moving of very heavy goods, as where a boiler-maker, or marine engineer, or locomotive-builder may have to hire special teams of horses to drag heavy loads to a wharf or railway station. Cases of this sort are rapidly diminishing in England, either by the closing of unprofitable factories or by the opening of new railways.

But while cartage may be saved by building a factory immediately on the railway, canal, river, or harbour which serves for transport, the convenience offered should not be over-estimated and allowed too great a weight against the opposing advantages of another site.

**Cartage costs little for light goods.**

The proportion which the expense of cartage bears to the total cost of production and delivery, differs of course with the nature of the trade. A manufacturer of light and valuable goods, if there be the general advantages of railway or canal carriage into the town or district, might find no sufficient inducement in the saving of cartage to draw him from an otherwise desirable site to one adjoining a railway.

**Railway sidings.**

A Railway Siding at a factory often enables a manufacturer to load and pack his goods more carefully or systematically than would be feasible at a common railway station, and in the case of heavy goods to utilise special cranes of the factory which do not exist at the station. Railway companies, however, do not always allow a reduction of charges corresponding to the duties of which they may be so relieved.

**Utilisation of waste products,**

The utilisation of Waste Products, which are necessarily localised, often determines the position of a factory; or the profits of the factory itself may depend upon the sale of its own bye-products. Thus, in large cities, factories find profitable employment in dealing with various kinds of refuse, while similar factories in less populous places would be quite unremunerative. Illuminating Gas can be made cheaply when the coke, pitch, oil, and ammonia find a ready sale; and as these sell best in considerable quantities, large cities have an advantage in the lower price of gas, of which London is an example.

**as in Gas making.**

**Contiguity to consumer.**

Contiguity to the Consumer is the circumstance that determines the locality of most factories, especially those of moderate extent. There are certain trades that are always necessary, and unless there be special difficulties in obtaining material or workmen, factories become established as the population reaches a certain point. This contiguity to the consumer is, in such cases, of greater importance than contiguous material, for the convenience to the purchaser of ready conference with the manufacturer, of examination of the goods, and of speedy delivery, may outweigh the mere saving in money which purchasing from the more distant factory might allow. The more successful or enterprising of such local manufacturers gradually acquire a trade with distant towns or with foreign countries; and, as the local customers thus become of less importance the question of removal to a locality more favourable for a wholesale or export trade arises. Sometimes manufacturers combine both methods, by retaining their offices and a small factory in the town where they are known, and establishing their principal factory in a more suitable place.

*See page* 78.

**Skilled workmen.**

Skilled Workmen may generally be best obtained in localities where there is a congregation of similar or kindred trades, as numerous factories create a good labour market and induce workmen to seek employment there. Such a congregation of factories also brings purchasers to the locality.

**Cheap labour remote from towns.**

It is expedient sometimes, in the case of certain trades, to choose a locality remote from a town, because labour may be obtained cheaply there, or because the workmen are less influenced by trades unions; but skilled workmen not unfrequently dislike factories remote from large towns, and prefer places where comforts and amusements are more abundant. A site otherwise desirable may be rendered useless for lack of Workmen's Houses, and if these have to be built for the purposes of the factory the capital expenditure becomes greatly increased. An expenditure for workmen's houses often proves a profitable investment for capital; but if the houses depend entirely on the new industry for tenants, a heavy pledge for its continuance is added to the general risks.

**Workmen's houses.**

*See page* 94.

**Subsidiary trades.**

Contiguity to Subsidiary Trades is sometimes of more consequence than at first appears. Thus, if a Birmingham gun factory, a Sheffield cutlery works, or a Nottingham lace mill could be transported with all its workmen to a district where materials were plentiful and a demand brisk for the commodities, but where no other similar factory existed, it might fail for want of the preliminary trades which perform cheaply, because exclusively, the earlier processes with the raw material, or certain finishing processes usually performed separately, for want of the adjunct or contributory trades for repairs and renewals, and for want of the various minor purveyors who surround the numerous similar factories in the original district, but which a single factory could not alone support. In other words, this subdivision of labour requires a large trade and a busy population; thus industries needing such contributory trades are difficult to transplant.

**Contiguity to fuel or power.**

Contiguity to Fuel or to Power may be absolutely necessary to allow of competition with rivals similarly favoured, but fuel is so cheap in England that except in metallurgical or chemical manufactures the cost does not greatly affect the choice of locality if other circumstances be favourable.

**Water supply.**

Water is necessary to most trades, quantity being important in some cases, as for washing ores or refrigerating; quality in others, as for paper-making and brewing; while the pressure from elevated reservoirs or from rapid streams is valuable as power. The Water Power of rivers or waterfalls is in some cases used with advantage instead of fuel power, and where a cheap or gratuitous source is available such an alternative is worth consideration. But where coal is cheap, as in England, it is only in rare cases that the advantages of water power balance the drawbacks to its use. Thus the locality may be inconvenient; and if in order to utilise water power, a factory has to be built in a place badly situated for materials, transport, subsidiary trades, workmen's houses or customers, such power, even if costing nothing in money, may be dearly bought. In order to render water power available, considerable expense in dams, reservoirs, conduits and sluices may be necessary; and the expense of these may quite outweigh

**Water power.** **Value restricted by cheaper fuel power.** **Expenses of water power.**

the capitalised equivalent of fuel consumed in a steam-engine. It is for these reasons rather than from inherent difficulties that the question of utilising tidal forces is postponed. Water power is liable to stoppage in dry seasons; and if a supplementary steam-engine has to be provided, much of the advantage of the water is lost. Water power is also liable to diminution by operations of drainage, or an increased consumption higher up the stream, involving possible disputes.

**Tidal forces.**

**Transmission of power by water.**

The above remarks do not touch on the question of the transmission by the accumulator or other water system, of power produced by a steam-engine or other original motor at a distance, such transmission being often convenient in or about a factory. And if new forms of storing and transmitting force cheaply by electricity or other means are invented, natural sources of water power will at once have an enhanced value, as they could then be utilised by factories placed in a convenient locality.

# INDEX.

LONDON: PRINTED BY WILLIAM CLOWES AND SONS, LIMITED,
STAMFORD STREET AND CHARING CROSS.

# OPINIONS OF THE PRESS ON THE FIRST EDITION.

## From THE SATURDAY REVIEW.

"All industrial works it need hardly be stated wear out sooner or later. For a while the machinery and buildings may show no signs of decay, and may appear even better than when first set up, just as the human machine gains in efficiency by practice and exercise; but not the less certain is it that each day that passes brings them nearer to the end of life.

"Unless owners would see the whole of their capital consumed and themselves bankrupt, they must make provision in time for meeting gradual decay. To impress this upon them and to discuss how the provision can best be made is the object of the little volume before us, which is written with knowledge and judgment. Mr. MATHESON discusses with some minuteness the various rates of depreciation that shall be allowed; and if the rules he lays down are carefully followed there will be very little room for error."

## From THE ENGINEER.

"The capital invested in factories in this country alone makes the subjects of Mr. MATHESON'S book of importance to a large class, and the want of information on the rates at which factories and plant depreciate, the numerous causes of variation in these rates, and the absence of agreement in the practice of arriving at or assigning them, renders Mr. MATHESON'S book important because it is a successful attempt to systematise existing information and to make it possible to arrive at something like uniformity and accuracy in the practice of making up balance sheets for valuations.

"A notable feature of the whole book is a most complete system of side index notes and page references to other parts of the book and to the curves and tables which give numerical value to the facts set forth.

"Though we might review this book at length, it will be sufficient to say that the work is unique of its kind and that no pains have been spared to make it really valuable to the very large class it addresses."

## From THE STATIST.

"The author in this work supplies auditors and accountants with some valuable data to enable them to properly deal with facts and figures as to the fair allotment to capital or revenue of actual expenditure or estimated depreciation. The work now before us deals concisely and clearly—first with the items of depreciation and next with valuation. The work as a whole deals with a practical subject in a practical manner."

## From THE LAW TIMES.

"Mr. MATHESON has succeeded in bringing together, within a small compass, a large amount of practical information of a kind which is not generally available, and it is therefore all the more valuable."

# *The History of Accounting*

*An Arno Press Collection*

Bennet[t], James [Arlington]. **The American System of Practical Book-Keeping** and Foster, B[enjamin] F[ranklin], **The Origin and Progress of Book-Keeping.** 1842/1852. Two vols. in one

Brief, Richard P., editor. **The Late Nineteenth Century Debate Over Depreciation, Capital and Income.** 1976

Brief, Richard P. **Nineteenth Century Capital Accounting and Business Investment.** 1976

Bruchey, Stuart W[eems]. **Robert Oliver and Mercantile Bookkeeping in the Early Nineteenth Century.** 1976

Church, A[lexander] Hamilton. **Production Factors in Cost Accounting and Works Management.** 1910

Cole, William Morse. **Accounts:** Their Construction and Interpretation for Business Men and Students of Affairs. 1908

Dicksee, Lawrence R[obert]. **Advanced Accounting.** 1903

Dicksee, Lawrence R[obert]. **Auditing:** A Practical Manual for Auditors. 1892

Dicksee, Lawrence R[obert]. **Auditing:** A Practical Manual for Auditors. Authorized American Edition, Edited by Robert H. Montgomery. 1905

Dicksee, Lawrence R[obert]. **Depreciation, Reserves, and Reserve Funds.** 1903

Dicksee, Lawrence R[obert] and Frank Tillyard. **Goodwill and Its Treatment in Accounts.** 1906

Folsom, E[zekiel] G[ilman]. **Folsom's Logical Bookkeeping:** The Logic of Accounts. 1873

Garcke, Emile and J[ohn] M[anger] Fells. **Factory Accounts, Their Principles and Practice.** 1893

Hatfield, Henry Rand. **Modern Accounting:** Its Principles and Some of its Problems. 1916

Kehl, Donald. **Corporate Dividends:** Legal and Accounting Problems Pertaining to Corporate Distributions. 1941

Leake, P[ercy] D[ewe]. **Depreciation and Wasting Assets and Their Treatment in Assessing Annual Profit and Loss.** 1912

Lisle, George. **Accounting in Theory and Practice.** 1900

Matheson, Ewing. **The Depreciation of Factories, Mines and Industrial Undertakings and Their Valuation.** 1893

Montgomery, Robert H. **Auditing Theory and Practice.** 1912

Norton, George Pepler. **Textile Manufacturers' Book-Keeping for the Counting House, Mill and Warehouse.** 1894

Paton, William A[ndrew] and Russell A[lger] Stevenson. **Principles of Accounting.** 1916

Pixley, Francis W[illiam]. **Auditors:** Their Duties and Responsibilities Under the Joint-Stock Companies Acts and the Friendly Societies and Industrial and Provident Societies Acts. 1881

Reiter, Prosper, Jr. **Profits, Dividends and the Law.** 1926

Scott, DR. **Theory of Accounts.** 1925

Scovell, Clinton H. **Interest as a Cost.** 1924

Sells, Elijah Watt. **The Natural Business Year and Thirteen Other Themes.** 1924

Soulé, Geo[rge]. **Soulé's New Science and Practice of Accounts.** 1903

Sprouse, Robert T[homas]. **The Effect of the Concept of the Corporation on Accounting.** 1976

Zeff, Stephen A., editor. **Asset Appreciation, Business Income and Price-Level Accounting: 1918-1935.** 1976